FRANCIS I

Books in the RENAISSANCE LIVES series explore and illustrate the life histories and achievements of significant artists, rulers, intellectuals and scientists in the early modern world. They delve into literature, philosophy, the history of art, science and natural history and cover narratives of exploration, statecraft and technology.

Series Editor: François Quiviger

Already published

FRANCIS I

The Knight-King

GLENN RICHARDSON

REAKTION BOOKS

For Roger Mettam,
In Memoriam

Published by Reaktion Books Ltd
2–4 Sebastian Street
London EC1V 0HE, UK
www.reaktionbooks.co.uk

First published 2025

EU GPSR Authorised Representative
Logos Europe, 9 rue Nicolas Poussin, 17000, La Rochelle, France
email: contact@logoseurope.eu

Printed and bound in India by Replika Press Pvt. Ltd

A catalogue record for this book is available from the British Library

ISBN 978 1 83639 121 0

COVER: Joos van Cleve, *Francis I*, c. 1532–3, oil on panel. Philadelphia
Museum of Art, PA (John G. Johnson Collection, 1917, Cat. 769).

CONTENTS

Introduction: Francis I, 'Renaissance' Monarch

The world had such a hope in his virtues and such an opinion
of his magnanimity and such a conceit of his judgement and
wit, that everyone confessed, that of very long time there
was none raised up to the crown with a greater expectation.
He was made the more agreeable to the fancies of men, by
the consideration of his age . . . his excellent feature and
proportion of body, his great liberality and general humanity
. . . But especially he pleased greatly the nobility, to whom he
transferred many singular and great favours.[1]

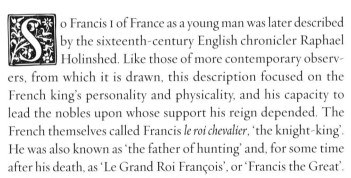 o Francis I of France as a young man was later described
by the sixteenth-century English chronicler Raphael
Holinshed. Like those of more contemporary observers, from which it is drawn, this description focused on the
French king's personality and physicality, and his capacity to
lead the nobles upon whose support his reign depended. The
French themselves called Francis *le roi chevalier*, 'the knight-king'.
He was also known as 'the father of hunting' and, for some time
after his death, as 'Le Grand Roi François', or 'Francis the Great'.

The king is now often described as the consummate 'Renaissance monarch', although what that means exactly is widely debated. At the very least, it means a monarch who was as committed
to the patronage of arts and education as he was to warfare, all

School of Jean Clouet, *Francis I*, c. 1515, oil on panel.

to the enhancement of his own authority and reputation, and the glorification of his dynasty.

This book presents the essentials of the king's life and reign, viewed from this perspective. The term 'Renaissance monarch' is a shorthand way of understanding how ancient ideals of kingship dating from the early medieval period were revived and, in a sense, reinvented in the fifteenth and sixteenth centuries during the period of the Italian, and wider European, Renaissance. Since medieval times, Western rulers had been regarded as semi-sacred beings, anointed and crowned by priests, and answerable to God for the authority entrusted to them. In exercising that authority, Francis and his contemporaries – notably Henry VIII of England, the Holy Roman Emperor Charles V and also Süleyman, the Sultan of the Ottomans – strove to have themselves regarded as three things: a great warrior, a great governor and a great patron in the widest sense of the term.

Almost regardless of the political and financial constraints they might face, rulers of the period sought to demonstrate personal valour and to have a significant presence on the international stage. War in the fifteenth and sixteenth centuries was usually undertaken for dynastic reasons, rather than what would today be called strategic or economic considerations, in the pursuit of personal reputation – what contemporaries called princely 'honour'. These monarchs also enjoyed quasi military sports, such as tournaments, hunting and archery, and spent hugely on these activities as a way of acting out their commitment to arms and their apparent prowess in warfare. In similar vein were the orders of chivalry, such as the Order of the Garter or the Golden Fleece, membership of which was prestigious. Leading the nobility and commanding in war in defence of the realm was still seen as the highest duty of a monarch. Francis subscribed to this view fully throughout his whole life, and he spent most of his reign at war, or managing its consequences in often complicated and expensive diplomacy. His principal aim in this respect was possession of the duchy of Milan and with it the region of Lombardy.

Monarchs of the Renaissance, like those of any era before it or since, expected to be obeyed and respected. The qualities of a good ruler were much debated in the period in many 'mirror for princes' treatises written for particular rulers. These include Erasmus's *The Education of a Christian Prince* and Machiavelli's *The Prince*, but there were many others, and at least two were written for Francis by scholar-courtiers. While all differed in their particular concerns, most of these tracts agreed that a capacity to maintain justice, law and order, and general good governance were key to successful monarchy. Kings had to deal with the major interest groups in their kingdoms, namely the religious and clerical establishment, the landed nobility, the nobles and gentry of their own legal administrations, merchants, municipal authorities and various representative assemblies from parliaments or estates to town councils. In an ideal world, the prince's own advisors, who formed his council, should be well educated and chosen for their commitment to the interests of the polity as a whole, not entirely those of the king, nor of themselves. They should offer the wisest, most honest advice possible, and all theorists agreed that flatterers were to be avoided. Needless to say, the extent to which these very high ideals were ever truly lived out anywhere may be a very different matter.

In the pre-modern period, there was a significant and evolving royal bureaucracy, although it was still very small by modern comparison. Growing numbers of lawyers and other specialists were entering crown service and developing its legal and fiscal machinery. The royal writ in France, as in other kingdoms, ran further than ever before. Politically, however, monarchs depended on nobles, gentry and non-titled subjects alike to cooperate with them to ensure the maintenance of law and order and good administration both nationally and locally. Grants of money, offices,

lands and titles could be made to individuals as inducements to cooperation or as payment. There was usually competition for the wealthiest official positions and sinecures, which often brought in train the potential to be close to the king himself, the fount of all favour and honours. Proximity could mean influence and the possibility of further rewards in royal service for individuals and their families and friends. All sensible leaders balanced such demands and rewards among the widest possible group of supporters, but most also relied on a favoured core of adherents with whom they interacted personally, within the princely court or royal household. There, people could form temporary alliances and groups to advance their interests, sometimes called factions, in an effort to enhance their own influence and deny others the same. Court life was therefore elegant, but also competitive and stressful. Francis led the trend in the sixteenth century for royal courts to become larger and more extravagant than before, identified by contemporaries as the virtue of 'magnificence', while also taking steps to give himself at times much-needed space among fewer adherents.

Salamander of Francis I, Château d'Azay-le-Rideau.

Francis's patronage was directed first and foremost at the social and economic elites of the kingdom, but it included legal and financial administrators, and political theorists. It also encompassed the artisans who made the monarch's clothes and armour, and created the silverware for his chapel and table, the accoutrements for his horses or the tapestries that decorated and insulated the court's reception rooms and the private royal apartments, to the most private of which only very privileged courtiers were admitted at will. Francis's patronage also encompassed, on a greater scale than before, artists and writers who, in paintings, sculptures, and poetry or prose, made images of the king that praised him in ways that enhanced his authority and appeal to the subjects upon whom he most closely depended. The imagery they created, displayed in the various court buildings Francis built or refurbished, drew on classical models of leadership, as did the fashionable political theories of the time. Francis was presented variously as, among many other things, Alexander the Great, Julius Caesar, Caesar Augustus and King David of the Israelites.

These themes will inform what follows. Francis saw himself as a king with the right, by virtue of his coronation oath, to direct the life of his realm directly. He was very conscious of his role as a governor as well as national leader, took it very seriously and expected to be obeyed without question, even if as a young man he often had difficulty in settling to the business of administration. He expected the support and cooperation of the ecclesiastical establishment and the nobles of France in maintaining his rights and assisting in his duties. When young, he was excited by warfare and extravagant diplomacy as he strove to make his name as the defender of France both within and beyond his kingdom. He expected to be able to use the wealth of the realm in this quest, but he had no idea when he began just how great that call would prove to be – something he regretted at the end of his life.

This, then, is the king presented here. More romanticized, and more hostile, accounts of him are available. This one seeks to interpret the essentials of his personality and style of kingship, so far as they may be recovered, comparing him with his contemporaries and, as far as the evidence allows, making sense of him in terms that he himself might have understood. That is, after all, the meaning of history. Francis seems to have been a man of sound and imaginative mind, who could display a winning generosity, even if he was also self-centred and often arrogant in his dealings with some of his subjects. He had an appreciation of physical life in all its forms, matched with a genuine appreciation of literature, the arts and the sciences. He was so driven by an ambition to be regarded as an exceptional king that it led him at times to risk not just his own life and livelihood, but potentially those of all his subjects, and the safety of the kingdom itself. He was authoritarian in outlook, but possessed a natural charisma to which many contemporaries attested. With all of that said, what will *you* make of him?

ONE

Le roi chevalier

On the Feast of the Conversion of St Paul 1515, my
son was anointed and consecrated in the Cathedral
of Rheims. For this, I am beholden to and acknowledge
Divine-Mercy, by which I have been amply recompensed
for all the adversities and troubles to which I was subject in
my earliest years, and in the flower of my youth: Humility
accompanied me, and Patience never abandoned me.[1]

obody, save his mother perhaps, ever thought Francis
would be king of France. The accession of Francis of
Angoulême to the throne was possibly the most unlikely of all in the history of the French monarchy. As his mother's reflection on his coronation attests, it seemed to require
divine intervention to bring it about. Sudden changes of fortune
were certainly necessary, and they occurred in the following
remarkable circumstances.

The boy who would be king was born to Louise de Savoie
(1476–1531) and her husband, Charles, comte d'Angoulême
(1459–1496), in the town of Cognac on the night of 12 September
1494. The house and *comté* (county or earldom) of Angoulême
was a junior branch of the Orléans dynasty, itself a cadet branch
of the royal house of Valois. Its founder was Charles's father, Jean
Orléans-Angoulême (1399–1467), who was a prince of royal blood

as grandson of Charles V of France (1338–1380), and who established his family seat at Cognac, on the Charente river. There he housed himself in a fine château with a substantial library.

The dynastic politics of King Louis XI (1423–1483) determined that Charles d'Angoulême should be betrothed to Louise, the daughter of Philippe, comte de Bresse, a younger son of the duc de Savoie, in order to prevent Charles d'Angoulême from being married to the daughter of Duke Charles the Bold of Burgundy (1433–1477), Louis' rival and enemy. Louise had been brought up at the court of her aunt, Louis' daughter Anne de Beaujeu (1461–1522). After the accession of Anne's younger brother Charles VIII (1470–1498), Charles d'Angoulême attempted unsuccessfully to get out of his betrothal to Louise, but Anne, as regent for the young Charles, insisted on the marriage. It finally took place on 16 February 1488. The couple had two children, their first a daughter, Marguerite (1492–1549), then Francis, who came along in 1494. His mother chose the name partly from a personal devotion to St Francis of Assisi, and much meaning would later be attributed to it for France itself, with punning allusions to 'frankness', freedom, openness and honesty. At the time of his birth, however, there was no expectation that Francis, although of royal blood and a cousin of the reigning monarch, would ever be king.

Charles d'Angoulême died on 1 January 1496, leaving Louise and his children with comparatively modest estates and means. His son's significance among his wider kin increased, however, when Louis II, duc d'Orléans (1462–1515), then leader of the Orléans clan, claimed the guardianship of the two Angoulême children on the grounds that Louise (still only nineteen) was a minor. This move was stoutly resisted by their mother, who was determined to play a direct role in raising them. A compromise was eventually reached whereby the technical legal guardianship of Francis and Marguerite was vested in Orléans, as the law required, while Louise had custody of them with responsibility for their day-to-day upbringing and education.

Charles VIII died suddenly in April 1498 and was succeeded by his cousin the aforementioned Louis d'Orléans, who reigned as Louis XII. Francis was Louis' first cousin once removed, but still his nearest male relative. He therefore became Louis' heir presumptive until the king should have a son of his own. In 1499 Louis made Francis duc de Valois and provided him with an annuity of 6,000 *livres*. The young duke continued to live with his mother and sister, but now the guardianship over him was given to Pierre de Rohan, seigneur de Gié (1451–1513), a Breton noble, a marshal of France and a powerful figure in Louis' regime. The king's intention was to keep Francis under Gié's close supervision as an important member of the Orléans branch of the royal dynasty. Charles VIII had been married to Anne de Bretagne (1477–1514), the daughter of the last independent duke of that duchy. The king of France had thereby established, in right of his wife, a dynastic claim on the duchy. Louis wished to secure that claim for himself, and, in order to do so, he now had his marriage to Jeanne de France (1464–1505) annulled so that he could marry Anne.

Medal of Louise of Savoy, countess of Angoulême, *c.* 1505, bronze.

Jeanne resisted at first but did not formally contest Louis' assertion that he had been forced into their marriage and that it had
never been consummated. Louis and Anne were married in January
1499, much to the consternation of Louise de Savoie, for it threatened her son's possible succession to the crown. Anne was soon
pregnant, and hopes were high of a son, but her first child was a
daughter, Claude, born in October 1499.

Louis suffered several bouts of serious illness in 1504–5. In
anticipation of the unspoken possibility of the king's death, Francis
lived intermittently at court during these years. Gié was disgraced after plausible allegations were made that he had tried
to assert too much control over the kingdom during Louis' illness.
The guardianship of Francis was transferred to Georges, Cardinal
d'Amboise (1460–1510). He was Louis' closest advisor, and the
cardinal's circle included a number of young men who would
become significant as royal advisors during the following reign.
Not least among these figures was Artus Gouffier, seigneur de
Boisy (c. 1474/5–1519), who was made governor of Francis's person
until he reached his majority.[2]

In light of these events, King Louis now determined that a
secure succession was paramount. As part of his effort to have
his claim to the duchy of Milan recognized by the Habsburg
dynasty, his eldest daughter, Claude (1499–1524), had been betrothed to Charles of Burgundy (1500–1558), the son of Duke
Philip of Burgundy (1478–1506) and grandson of the Holy
Roman Emperor Maximilian I von Habsburg (1459–1519). Now,
in May 1506, that engagement was abrogated and Claude was
betrothed instead to Francis. The ceremony took place at Tours
before the great and good of the realm. It was conducted by
Cardinal d'Amboise as an act of the highest national and dynastic importance, and with good reason. Had Claude and Charles
of Burgundy ever married, the accession of their Habsburg heir
would have tested the Salic law and had profound consequences

for France and for sixteenth-century Europe more widely. Instead, Claude's betrothal to Francis affirmed for the future the primacy of the cadet house of Orléans-Angoulême in the succession to the Valois crown, and secured its connection to Brittany into the next generation.

In August 1508, as Francis's fourteenth birthday approached and he became technically capable of assuming the kingship should it be required of him, he moved permanently to the royal court, 'leaving me all alone', as Louise de Savoie noted plaintively in her journal.[3] The following year, Marguerite was married to Charles IV, duc d'Alençon (1489–1525), at the behest of Louis XII. From about this time Francis began to be addressed by the courtesy title of 'dauphin' and was admitted to the royal council. Louis seems reluctantly to have accepted that Francis needed some education in the rudiments of governance. Yet he did not repose much confidence in the teenage prince, whom he thought temperamentally unsuited to kingship. 'This big boy will ruin everything,' he is recorded as saying on more than one occasion. The king's second child, his daughter Renée, was born in October 1510. On 21 January 1512, at the end of what proved to be her last pregnancy, Queen Anne was finally delivered of a son, but he was either stillborn or died almost immediately. Louise de Savoie was as relieved at this news as she was exultant.

In addition to holding on to Brittany, Louis had been determined from the start of his reign to wrest the duchy of Milan from Ludovico Sforza (1452–1508). Louis' claim to the duchy derived from the pre-existing line of Visconti dukes. This was based on the marriage, in 1389, of Valentina Visconti (1371–1408), the daughter of Gian Galeazzo Visconti (1351–1402), then duke of Milan, to Louis I, duc d'Orléans (1372–1407), a younger brother of King Charles VI of France. She and Louis had sons, the eldest of whom, Charles (1394–1465), was a noted late medieval poet. He theoretically succeeded to Milan at his father's death in 1407 and to the county of Asti at the death of his mother a year later, in 1408. Before he was able to do anything about this claim, however, Charles was captured at the Battle of Agincourt in 1415, and spent many years as a prisoner in England. Charles's son Louis d'Orléans (thus Valentina's grandson), as Louis XII, claimed the title of Milan in right of his grandmother. This claim was contested by Maximilian I, who had his own claim to Milan through his marriage into the Sforza family, members of which had overthrown the Visconti in Milan. In 1494 Ludovico Sforza sought recognition as the legitimate duke of Milan from Maximilian. To secure this, his niece Bianca Maria Sforza (1472–1510), the eldest legitimate daughter of Duke Galeazzo Maria Visconti and Bona of Savoy, was married to the Austrian ruler who was elected king of the Romans in 1486 and proclaimed himself Holy Roman Emperor in 1508. Maximilian asserted this claim of right on Milan through the Sforza, and in turn passed it to his own grandson Charles V.

In August 1499 Louis XII invaded and occupied the duchy of Milan with an army under the command of the Milanese-born *condottiere* Gian Giacomo Trivulzio (*c.* 1440–1518). In 1512 the

Medal of Francis, duke of Valois, *c.* 1505, bronze.

king sought to strengthen his hold on the duchy and to widen French influence in Lombardy and beyond. This led to a dispute with Pope Julius II (1443–1513), who opposed French intervention. In the course of this clash, Louis was excommunicated and a war began under the pope's aegis, into which Henry VIII of England (1491–1547) was drawn. In the summer of 1512 Henry sent an army to invade southwestern France in alliance with his father-in-law Ferdinand II of Aragon (1452–1516). Ferdinand diverted Henry's forces to help him overrun the kingdom of Navarre, on the border with Spain, and the emperor joined the war as well.

Pope Julius II died in February 1513 and was succeeded in March by Giovanni de' Medici (1475–1521) as Pope Leo X. The new pontiff spent the remainder of 1513 establishing his court and overseeing the restoration of his family to power in Florence, but he made it known that he favoured peace. Even as the new pope was finding his feet, a Swiss army forced the French out of Milan and an uprising installed Massimiliano Sforza (1493–1530), succeeding his father, Ludovico. Louis counter-attacked, but on 6 June his army was defeated at the Battle of Novara. The same month a new phase of the war began in northern France. Henry VIII personally invaded with a huge army. His campaign culminated in the conquest of the city of Tournai. By the end of 1513 Louis had been fought to a standstill on all sides, and plans were in hand for a new phase of attack on France the following year. As if all this were not enough for Louis, on 9 January 1514 Queen Anne died at Blois, aged only 37. While Louis still hoped to marry again to secure an heir, this seemed unlikely. He there-fore ordered that the marriage of Claude and Francis should now go ahead, and in May that year the wedding took place at Saint-Germain-en-Laye. It seemed Louis had finally accepted that he would now be succeeded by Francis.

After the election of Leo X, Louis had worked assiduously to be reconciled with the new pope. Generous peace terms were also offered to Ferdinand of Aragon and Maximilian to end their campaigns against him, and, the quarrel with the pope resolved, they soon did so. As we have seen, Louis had hoped to have his claims to Milan recognized by Maximilian, partly through substituting in marriage to Charles of Burgundy his youngest daughter, Renée, for her older sister Claude, who had just married Francis. Henry VIII was abruptly abandoned by his two allies, but Louis quickly offered him generous peace terms, based on the renewal of the huge annual pension the kings of France had paid to their English counterparts since the time of Edward IV. Henry was initially reluctant to make peace, but Louis found willing assistance from Henry's foremost advisor, Thomas Wolsey (c. 1472/5–1530), then bishop of Lincoln and Tournai, who was already showing a talent for grandiose diplomacy. Wolsey negotiated the first Treaty of London, signed on 7 August 1514, whereby Henry agreed not just to peace but also to a full Anglo-French alliance. Louis was delighted that it was to be secured by his betrothal to Henry's eighteen-year-old sister, Mary (1496–1533), already a renowned beauty. The alliance was a volte-face for these two traditional enemies, and it rapidly became the talk of Europe. It disconcerted not only Ferdinand, but Maximilian and Pope Leo. Having almost given up hope, the 52-year-old Louis now had another chance of producing a son with whom to displace Francis. Louise de Savoie was *not* amused.

Amid splendid ceremonies and entertainments, Mary was married to Louis at Abbeville on 9 October 1514. She was crowned Queen of France in the basilica of Saint-Denis on the northern outskirts of Paris on 5 November, the only Englishwoman in history ever to be so crowned. Francis attended Mary at her coronation ceremony, and led her formal entry into Paris as queen the following day. He spent hugely on the tournament held in her honour at the Hôtel des Tournelles. If the young duke had any misgivings at the arrival of the woman, two years his junior, whose longed-for child might yet deprive him of the crown, he did not show them. His demeanour sprang from a personal confidence, even assurance, that the king was either too old or too ill to procreate, or so he confided to his friend Robert III de La Marck, seigneur de Florange (1491–1537). At the very least, Francis knew he would hereafter play a prominent role in the future of the French state, and so did the English. Thomas Howard, 2nd Duke of Norfolk (1443–1524), led Mary Tudor's escort to France; he observed to Wolsey, 'here is nothing done but the said duke is made privy and doer thereof by the French king's commandment,' adding, 'My Lord, I assure you this prince can speak well and wisely.'⁴ Louis was rejuvenated by his marriage, or was elaborately careful to appear so. The age difference between them notwith-standing, the couple were publicly affectionate. Nevertheless, despite her attentions (or, as some satirists suggested, because of them), Louis' health declined rapidly during December. He remained in Paris, was unwell over Christmas and was reported to be *in extremis* as the new year approached.

Then, suddenly, it happened. Louis XII died on the night of Monday, 1 January 1515. At that moment, Francis became the king of France. Louise received the news within hours at her home at Romorantin in the Loire Valley. She set off by torchlight in the early hours of Wednesday, 3 January to be with her son, at the heart of whose regime she would remain until her own death sixteen years later. In accordance with the custom that 'the king never dies', Francis neither oversaw nor attended his predeces-sor's funeral on 12 January.⁵ Mary Tudor, forever after known to the English as the 'French Queen', was sent to the abbey of Cluny for a month's confinement formally to determine whether she was pregnant. Any son born within a year and a day of Louis' death would be his successor. Yet Mary told Francis plainly that she knew she was not pregnant, and he proceeded with arrangements for his coronation.

The splendid ceremony took place in the cathedral of Rheims on 25 January 1515. Francis swore to uphold the Catholic faith, to protect the Church and the realm, and to rule with justice and equity. Having taken the oath, he was anointed with holy oil kept in a special ampulla at Rheims. It was believed to be self-replenishing and initially bestowed by the Holy Spirit for the coronation of Clovis as the first Christian king of France. This anointing conferred a sacerdotal or semi-priestly status on the king – hence in part the word *sacre* to describe the coronation ritual. Then, clothed with a magnificent blue gown embroidered all over with gold fleurs-de-lis, Francis received from the archbishop of Rheims the ring, the sword, the sceptre and a special rod, 'the hand of justice', all symbols of different aspects of his sovereignty and commitment to the realm of France. The high point came when the king was crowned with the crown of Charlemagne and recognized by the peers of France. The trumpets and drums sounded, together with the great organ of the cathedral. Enthroned before the huge congregation, and in the presence of his mother, Francis was acclaimed as king with cries of 'Vivat Rex' and 'Vive le roi'.

'RAISED UP TO THE CROWN'

The kingdom of France that Francis inherited was somewhat smaller than present-day France, but was already becoming the large, unitary, royal state it would be in the following centuries, a process to which the king contributed directly. Francis ruled over some 15 million people, who inhabited a land area of about 459,000 square kilometres (177,200 sq. mi.). There were wide variations of income, education and outlook between, and within, the three estates into which French society organized itself. There were also regional and cultural variations, not least in language. The *langue d'oïl* – from which modern French comes – was generally spoken in the north, and the *langue d'oc* (or Occitan) in the south and east, and there were numerous dialects. There were also still significant areas that were independent of the crown, such as Brittany, or which recognized the king of France in some other capacity, such as Provence. The English still held the Pale of Calais in the northwest and the Chalon-Arlay family held the independent principality of Orange in Provence.

People did move for work, better wages or other life opportunities, and the number of towns grew in the sixty-odd years between the end of the Hundred Years War and Francis's accession. It has been estimated that there were about two hundred cities and towns in early sixteenth-century France, from the smallest with populations of 5,000 people or so, up to the four regional cities of Lyon, Orléans, Rouen and Toulouse, with up to 70,000 residents. Above them all was Paris, the royal capital and, by some estimates, the largest European city during Francis's reign, with a population well over 100,000. It was the major centre of commerce and banking, manufacturing and printing, as well as housing the principal educational, administrative and judicial institutions of the kingdom. Francis maintained generally good, but sometimes restive, relations with the city's authorities and elites and, unlike his predecessors, from 1527 spent more time in or near Paris than anywhere else in the kingdom. This made the city even more significant as the principal site of the royal court, although Francis continued to travel widely in his domain until his final years.

How prepared to govern this large kingdom was Francis, the 'unexpected' king? He was certainly well educated as a nobleman by contemporary standards. In *The Book of the Courtier* (1528), Baldassare Castiglione praised the young French nobleman's intellectual and artistic development. One of his characters, Magnifico Giuliano, says of Francis:

For when I was at Court not so long ago, I set eyes on this prince, and it seemed to me that besides his handsome looks, there was such an air of greatness about him, accompanied, however, with a certain gracious humility, that the kingdom of France on its own must always seem too limited for him. And subsequently from many gentlemen both French and Italian, I heard a great deal in praise of his noble courtesy, his magnanimity, his valour and his generous spirit; and among other things was told that he greatly loved and esteemed learning and respected all men of letters and that he condemned the French themselves for being hostile to this profession, especially as they have in their midst as magnificent a university as Paris, where people flock from all over the world.[6]

The pattern of his education is, however, hard to trace in detail. As we have seen, Charles d'Angoulême had built up the collection of his father's library at Cognac and patronized a number of poet-historians known as *rhétoriqueurs*. Using these and other resources, Louise had taught both children their essential literary skills, the basic elements of Latin, Italian and Spanish. She is also known to have commissioned several books that were dedicated to her and used in her children's intellectual development. Francis may also have studied with the Flemish humanist scholar Christophe de Longueil, although the evidence for this is equivocal. More certainly, Louise employed one François Demoulins as tutor. A Franciscan abbot and Christian humanist reformist, Demoulins wrote several treatises associated with Francis's education, the most famous of which is probably *Dialogus* (1505) on the morals of games of chance. With him, the future king developed his knowledge of Latin and probably also Greek. Demoulins was still active in Francis's education and early literary patronage as late as 1513, and was made *Grand Aumônier* (Grand Chaplain) of France in 1519, with formal responsibility for the king's chapel and his charitable giving, although these functions were carried

out by others. The *Journal* of Louise de Savoie was not, as its title
suggests, written by her daily, but rather was a form of memoir,
probably written up by Demoulins from notes made by Louise.
Its obsessive references to Louise's love for Francis flattered her
as a mother, and her son as king. They capture the spirit of her
expressed feelings on particular occasions, but the journal was
primarily intended to promote the idea of Francis's providential
accession, reflect on the key points on his path to the throne and
record the main personal events of his early years as king.[7]

Through his mother's guidance and that of his tutors, Francis
developed a genuine admiration for classical languages and philosophy and a wish to patronize humanist scholarship, although
the depth and security of his own learning have often been debated.
He was a poor Latinist but did evidently develop an appreciation
of Greek as he matured. One of the earliest scholars under royal
patronage was Guillaume Budé (1467–1540), the king's first secretary, later keeper of the royal library at Fontainebleau, and France's
foremost Hellenist, who wrote a treatise on kingship for Francis
in the early years of the young king's reign. Marguerite was more
learned than her younger brother. She became an important poet
in her own right, the author of the *Heptaméron*, a collection of
stories modelled on Giovanni Boccaccio's mid-fourteenth-century
Decameron. She was also a lifelong patron of humanist learning and
evangelical theology, most prominently in the early 1530s. Her
spiritual poem *Miroir de l'âme pécheresse* (Mirror of the Sinful Soul)
was studied and translated by the future Elizabeth I as part of her
education (although it had been banned by the Faculty of Theology
of the University of Paris in 1533). Francis was intrigued by the natural sciences and astronomy, and developed a genuine connois-
seurship, unrivalled by any of his immediate royal contemporaries,
in painting, sculpture and architecture. He had a reputation, even
as quite a young man, as a lively conversationalist who could
address a range of subjects with obvious intelligence.

Louise de Savoie and Charles d'Angoulême playing chess, miniature by
Robinet Testard from Evrart de Conty, *Livre des échecs amoureux moralisés*, 1496–8.

While literature was to the fore, other aspects of the future king's education as a nobleman were not neglected. In common with his contemporaries, he was taught the expected equestrian skills and practised swordsmanship. As a young man, Francis stood just over 2 metres (6 ft 2 in.) tall. He was physically strong and naturally disposed to strenuous sports of all kinds, particularly the quasi-martial pursuits of the tournament and, above all else, hunting. With his height and athletic build, he was thus something of a jock and, even into early middle age, prided himself on his masculine strength. As a young man particularly, however, this was an important aspect of the projection of his legitimacy as monarch. He was literally fit for the job, and took every opportunity to display his physical prowess in sport and in dancing, rather as did his English counterpart Henry – of whose reputation as a superb sportsman Francis was well aware.[8] Francis was described by the English chronicler Edward Hall as being, in 1520, 'a goodly prince, stately of countenance, merry of cheer, brown coloured, great eyes, high nosed, big lipped, fair breasted and shoulders, small [thin] legs and long feet'. Another chronicler, Ellis Griffith, who saw him at the Field of Cloth of Gold that year, described him as being 2 metres (6 ft) tall, with brown hair neatly combed, a broad neck and a dark beard. Griffith noted the king's long 'Valois' nose (as Hall had done) and his hazel eyes, although he thought the king's complexion fair rather than otherwise.[9]

Francis had gained limited experience of warfare before his accession. In September 1512 he was the captain of a company of one hundred lances, mounted men-at-arms. He was appointed titular commander of the royal army sent to retake Navarre from Ferdinand of Aragon. In view of the dauphin's youth and inexperience, the operational commander was Odet de Foix, vicomte de Lautrec (c. 1481–1528), with whose family Francis would have close association as king. Francis was involved in the organization of the army at least, but saw no significant action. He was again in titular command the following year against Henry of England, and his banner was one of those captured at the Battle of the Spurs in August 1513, although he was not himself on the field at the time. Nevertheless, his participation in his first war was commemorated with a bronze medal, featuring Francis in classical profile, a victor's circlet of laurel leaves around his head. Presumably commissioned by his mother or someone in her circle, the medal is inscribed *Maximus Franciscus Francorum Dux 1512*. The title 'duke of the French' was formally meaningless but, with the laurel leaves, powerfully associated Francis as heir presumptive with an 'imperial' kingdom of France. He is often referred to as 'mon César' in Louise's journal. What Louis XII had made of this Angoulême family pretentiousness at the time may easily be imagined.

After his coronation, Francis went to the priory of Corbény to visit the shrine of St Marcoul, who was associated with the healing powers believed to be granted to the kings of France. Francis also visited the shrine of the Black Virgin at Notre-Dame de Liesse, then journeyed by easy stages to Compiègne. In the days and weeks that followed, the monarch busied himself in making a range of new appointments, and confirming many existing ones, in his household and wider administration. The key figure at Francis's accession was Artus Gouffier de Boisy, his former governor, who took charge of the royal household as *Grand maître* (Great Master) of France. Twenty years older than the new king, Boisy did not come from a family of ancient lineage, but various relatives had made advantageous marriages into older families, including the Amboise seigneurs de Chaumont, and the Montmorency. He brought his brother Guillaume (*c.* 1488–1525), eight years his junior, into his protégé's circle alongside his other childhood companions Anne de Montmorency (1493–1567) and Robert III de La Marck.[10] Guillaume received a present of 1,000 crowns and was made Admiral of France. Florimond Robertet (*c.* 1460–1527), Louis' secretary of finances, retained his post, bringing a much-needed continuity of experience to the royal council. New blood was infused with the appointment as chancellor of Antoine Duprat (1463–1535), president of the *Parlement* of Brittany and a supporter of Louise de Savoie. Francis also brought into his regime one of the most powerful nobles in France, Charles III, duc de Bourbon (1490–1527). The Bourbon family were princes of the blood and had several branches of which Charles's was, by marriage, the most senior. Francis recognized Charles's status, and his notable service record in Italy under Louis XII, by making him the Constable of France, the chief military officer of the realm after the king himself. Their relations were always cordial rather than warm, but Bourbon served Francis as well as he had Louis before him.

One of Francis's first acts as newly crowned monarch was to erect his family's earldom of Angoulême to a duchy, in favour of his mother. He also gave Louise the duchy of Anjou, together with the earldoms of Maine and Beaufort-en-Vallée and the supporting barony of Amboise, making her not only the most powerful but, by some way, one of the richest women in France.[11] She was then 38 years old and was described in 1517 by Antonio de Beatis, the secretary of the Cardinal of Aragon, who saw her at Rouen, as tall, well complexioned and lively: 'She always accompanies her son and the queen and plays the governess without restraint.' Her near presence to Francis and that of his sister ruffled patriarchal sensibilities in France and beyond, with accusations that so masculine a figure as Francis was 'effeminate' in the original sense of being too much with and influenced by women. This found echoes in the account of Francis by some nineteenth-century historians. Marguerite's husband, Charles d'Alençon, as a prince of the blood and Francis's nearest male relative, was nominated as his heir and known as 'the second person of the kingdom'.[12]

It was before the great nobles and the bourgeois elite of the city that Francis made his formal entry into Paris as king on

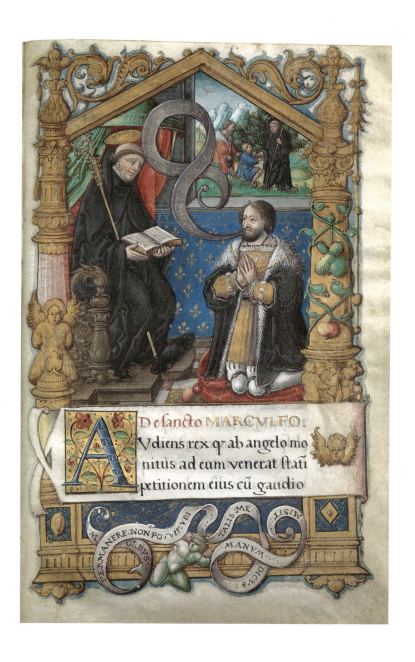

Francis I before St Marcoul, miniature from the Hours of Francis I by the Master of François de Rohan, c. 1539–40.

15 February 1515. He was received by representatives of the city's government, its trade and commercial guilds, the clergy, the university and the sovereign law court, the *Parlement* of Paris. Prominently on display in the procession was the king's personal emblem of the salamander amid flames. According to Ovid, the salamander's amphibious cold-blooded nature allowed it to live in fire. It had been an Angoulême family symbol for some time, and the royal salamander was nearly always shown spitting jets of water from its mouth. It was supported by a motto, *nutrisco et extinguo*, generally rendered as 'I nourish the good and extinguish evil.' Together, the emblem and motto conveyed the idea that the king was inflamed by his passionate nature, but was also able to contain and direct that energy for the best. He sustained and nourished his subjects and friends but repressed his enemies.[13] In this and other ways, Francis's youth and ambition were publicly welcomed in the ceremonies.

Yet his inexperience was also commented upon immediately in France and beyond. The University of Paris gave the traditional accession oration, which flattered his youthful attractiveness and imputed to him a willingness to take advice and uphold the good lordship of his royal predecessors.[14] It expresses what might be called the 'establishment' attitude to someone who was, according to contemporary understanding, still an adolescent ruler. That is, although he was a twenty-year-old king in full sovereignty and a married man, he was still young and still apt to be governed and trained by older people. He inherited a royal council whose advice he was expected at least to consider carefully. Such councils to a young king tended to keep him in a sort of tutelage or apprenticeship until he found a way to assert the reality of his 'personal rule' for himself. They tended to want to maintain his predecessor's policies, or were at least wary of novelty. Naturally gregarious and charismatic, Francis (like his English counterpart Henry) much preferred to hunt and enjoy 'pastime with good company' than to engage in the tedious business of council meetings. The prominent men of the council, and Louise de Savoie, constituted the core of the government of France, whose society was comparatively free and open, if still strictly hierarchical, when Francis was king.

The bulk of the population, whether in rural or urban areas, comprised what was called the third estate. It included more or less anyone who was not a member of the clergy or a noble, the first and second estates respectively. The vast majority of French people lived in the countryside in one of the estimated 30,000 villages, working the fields as peasants, pursuing such artisanal trades as baking, carpentry and stonemasonry, or earning a living in service. They lived under a local landlord or *seigneur*. Arable land was still plentiful and comparatively cheap at the end of the fifteenth century. The rents and dues the landlord earned from holdings could be numerous and lucrative or quite small, providing only enough for a family to live without themselves labouring. There were also village councils or assemblies that were responsible for the local upkeep, and who worked with the crown's officials to raise royal taxes, such as the *taille* in its various forms, which was used for the defence of the realm. Such councils were often dominated by the tradesmen of the village and the *fermiers*, men who owned some land and perhaps employed a few others – something like the yeomanry in England.

There were perhaps some 100,000 ordinary members of the clergy, from humble parish priests to orders of monks and friars who lived in more than 11,000 religious houses of many kinds. As elsewhere in Europe, this estate was supervised by the hierarchy of bishops, archbishops and cardinals, and relations with these authorities and the papacy were important in the government and security of France. The nobles comprised individuals defined by birth and inheritance, or by act of ennoblement by the king. They constituted a wide range of people, from the poorest village *hobereaux* in the provinces to the great aristocrats, and as a group they held the greater proportion of France's landed wealth. Exempt from direct taxation in return, originally, for service in war, 'sword' nobles had been growing slightly in number over the course of a century before Francis. Alongside the old nobility were royal office-holders, judges, secretaries and some other officials, called 'robe' nobles after their long black or red gowns. Their numbers increased markedly under Francis, but not as quickly as under his successors. The aim of many of these lawyers, financial officials and merchants was to get themselves accepted – through marriages and/or the acquisition of seigneuries – into the circle of more ancient landed families and to 'live nobly' from landed estates.[15]

THE LURE OF ITALY

Francis considered that the best way to demonstrate his aptitude for kingship and to build personal support among the nobles across his kingdom might be to uphold all the complex dynastic claims he had inherited from Louis, both as head of the house of Orléans and as king of France. First and foremost, this meant regaining the duchy of Milan and with it most of Lombardy, which, before his death, Louis had been preparing to invade again. Francis himself was also descended from Valentina Visconti through his grandfather, her son Jean d'Angoulême, so his marriage to Claude united both the Orléans dynasty's claims to Milan. The French nobility seemed keen to support Francis, but he faced considerable opposition from the incumbent duke Massimiliano Sforza together with Louis' old adversaries, Ferdinand of Aragon and Emperor Maximilian. They were now joined in alliance by Pope Leo X and a number of the cantons of the Swiss Confederation, now exercising a freedom and international influence long fought for against Austria and the Holy Roman Empire. All wanted to keep the new French king out of Milan and the Italian peninsula.

Faced with these unpropitious circumstances, Boisy advised Francis to keep the peaceful relations with the Habsburgs that Louis had, until 1512, generally maintained. The States-General of the Netherlands was already so well aware of Francis's military potential that, within two months of his accession, it had asked Charles of Burgundy (1500–1558), the future emperor, to accept full sovereignty over his Burgundian patrimony in right of his father, but which was then under the authority of his grandfather Maximilian. Charles agreed, wanting to assert himself against Francis, but he was not in a position to do so militarily at this point and was now vassal to the king of France for the counties of Flanders and Artois. Accordingly, peace was agreed through the Treaty of Paris of 24 March 1515, according to which the king's sister-in-law Renée de France (1510–1575) was confirmed as Charles's future bride.[16]

Francis also wanted to secure peace with Henry of England. His effort was both helped and hindered by a minor scandal that arose over the secret marriage of Mary Tudor to Charles Brandon, Duke of Suffolk (1484–1545), in Paris in February 1515. Suffolk, Henry's close companion, had been sent to congratulate Francis on his accession and to escort Mary home. The feisty youngest Tudor had insisted on immediate marriage to Brandon, to secure her own future as she wanted it. Francis created a diplomatic incident, hoping to embarrass Henry into conceding Tournai (captured in 1513) in return for his discreet and peaceable handling of a development about which he had every right to be angry. As dowager queen, Mary was (at least technically) one of his subjects, and required his permission to marry again. He even wanted Suffolk to conduct the negotiations over Tournai. It was now, however, that Francis first learned how formidable was Cardinal Wolsey's influence over Henry's international relations.

Wolsey intervened directly, telling Francis to forget the idea of an immediate return of Tournai. It would be returned to him only in exchange for a binding and restricting alliance with Henry – something Francis was at that moment anxious to avoid. The most Francis finally secured was a renewal of the existing peace with England, but if it held it would suit his purposes well enough. The special ambassador sent to convey the news that Suffolk and Mary were pardoned was Sir Thomas Boleyn. During his embassy he secured for his youngest daughter, Anne, a place as *demoiselle d'honneur* in Queen Claude's household.[17]

Francis was, however, able to secure a very important ally during the first months of the year. The Republic of Venice, then the most powerful Italian state, had been at odds with Louis XII since his armies had defeated its forces at Agnadello in 1509, as part of the League of Cambrai. Venice was wary of Francis but, hoping to make a fresh start with the new king, agreed to support him in return for his support against Emperor Maximilian and the papacy. The Venetians had learned from their narrow escape in 1509 and now engaged competent military commanders who more willingly closed with the enemy, rather than just manoeuvring about them while awaiting a political deal, as had often been the pattern of Italian warfare in the previous century. This would soon prove crucial to Francis's fortunes.

Having secured this ally and France's borders as best he could, in late April Francis journeyed with Queen Claude south along the Seine and then the Loire, into the valley that was then the homeland of the Valois monarchy. The queen was already pregnant with her first child. Arriving at Blois, the royal couple made their formal entry into the town and took possession of a château there much loved by Louis XII, Anne de Bretagne and Claude. There, Louis had first introduced elements of classical decoration into his architectural projects. His equestrian statue, with allusions to the Roman emperor Marcus Aurelius and his own conquest of Milan, can still be seen over the gateway of the essentially Gothic wing that he built at the château. Francis commissioned plans for a new wing that still bears his name, and which took classicism literally to new heights in France. Its main feature is the facade of loggias on the side looking out over the royal gardens (and once connected to them by a gallery). Although clearly inspired by contemporary Italian models, the loggias are not regularly spaced and sit below a traditional French dormer roof, and the wing perhaps looks a little squashed. However, the loggias were the first to be built on this scale in France. This unprecedented monumentality is carried further in the most famous feature of the castle, the external staircase on the main court, which gives access to the royal apartments. It is an impressive, fully articulated structure combining real understanding of design with a mix of classical and traditional Gothic motifs in the decoration – not least Francis's salamanders. Francis also began work at this time on what became the château of Chambord, although this did not progress significantly for a decade or more.

From Blois, Francis moved the short distance to Amboise and remained there into the early summer of 1515. On 26 June the king and queen attended the wedding of Renée de Bourbon (1494–1539), the Constable's sister, to Antoine, duc de Lorraine (1489–1544). Five years older than Francis, Antoine had befriended the future king at Louis' court. He had fought at Agnadello and would soon accompany Francis to Italy. As part of the celebrations, a boar hunt was staged in the enclosed courtyard of the château. All the exits were blocked off but the boar, terrified and maddened by the pursuit, broke through the barriers and came charging up the staircase from the top of which the king and the royal party were watching the spectacle. With perfect composure – or so we are assured – Francis arose, sword in hand, and, with a single powerful stroke into the body, stopped the unfortunate animal, which tumbled back down the stairs into the courtyard, dead.[18]

There is no reason to doubt the story, which shows how physically strong and brave Francis was, demonstrating his presence of mind in a dangerous situation.

By then, Francis was an experienced huntsman. Hunting became his lifelong preferred form of leisure. He hunted not simply because he enjoyed it and was very good at it, but also to show his skill at the chase to ambassadors and courtiers alike. His expenditure reflected this. From a total cost of 32,869 *livres* in various related departments of the household in 1518, it rose by some 71 per cent to almost 58,000 *livres* per annum between 1542 and 1546.[19] The king's horses were under the supervision of the *Grand Écuyer* (Master of the Horse), the Milanese nobleman Galeazzo da San Severino (*c.* 1460–1525).[20] For horses, Francis looked principally to Mantua and the coursers bred on the Gonzaga estates there. Lighter than the Neapolitan ones, they were cross-bred with Barbary and Turcoman stock. The rest of the hunting establishment was supervised by the *Grand Veneur*. From 1526 this was Claude de Lorraine, duc de Guise (1496–1550).[21]

A few days after the dramatic encounter with the boar at Amboise, Queen Claude, as the daughter of Louis XII, formally made her inherited claim to Milan over to her husband. During the days that followed, looking out from the parapets of Amboise over the fast-flowing river below the castle and the hunting forest beyond, Francis began planning the first military campaign of his reign. He had naturally decided from the outset to lead his army personally. He was accompanied by three of the four marshals of France, including Trivulzio, who had taken Milan for Louis, and Jacques de Chabannes, seigneur de La Palice (1470–1525). The army of some 40,000 was led by the heavy cavalry of about 2,500 noblemen. Known as the *gendarmerie*, it was paid for by a personal tax, the *taille royal* introduced by Charles VII. It was organized into *compagnies d'ordonnance*. Under the command of a noble captain appointed by the king himself, each cavalry company was formed

of a number of 'lances'. Each lance comprised a mounted man-at-arms in full plate armour, a sword-bearing 'coutillier', a page, two mounted archers and a valet, so that the fighting power of each lance was three or four men. They had eight horses between them. The king also commanded two companies of mounted royal guards, the Scots Guard and the *Cent gentilshommes* (100 Gentlemen) of the household. Other mounted troops were raised by the feudal levy upon which the king was entitled to call in time of war.[22]

For infantry, like Louis before him, Francis relied on a force of some 23,000 volunteers, raised mainly from Picardy, Gascony and the Basque country, known as the *franc archers*, together with about 17,000 German mercenary troops, the *Landsknechts*, raised from imperial territories. This included about 6,000 men formerly in the employ of the emperor but now forming 'the Black Band', commanded by Charles II, Duke of Guelders (1467–1538), an ally

Château of Blois, Francis I wing.

of Francis. Like their Swiss equivalents, *Landsknechts* fought in squares
with long pikes and, in close combat, with swords and daggers.
There were also about four hundred *arquebusiers*. The *arquebus* or
hackbut was a large hand-held weapon that was gradually evolving
into the musket (the ancestor of the modern rifle) and was increasingly used by infantry and on horseback, replacing the crossbow.
In support, Francis had one of the largest artillery forces in Europe,
comprising about 72 heavy cannon of different calibres, and lighter
hand cannon and the *arquebuses*. The field artillery had been developed in the course of fighting the English in the 1440s and '50s.
It was mounted on carriages for easy transportation and deployment, and used variously in sieges and on the battlefield. It was
under the overall command of Jacques de Genouillac *dit* Galiot
(1465–1546), a veteran soldier who had fought with Charles VIII
and Louis XII on their Italian campaigns, in which artillery had
played an important strategic, and occasionally tactical, part.[23]

In July Francis made a splendid entry into Lyon. The city
greeted him with decorations and celebrations that quite deliberately rivalled those of Paris. Lyon saw itself as at least the equal
of the royal capital in ancient lineage, in wealth and in political
importance. The city presented itself to Francis as loyal to him
and simultaneously as the headquarters of the Constable and
the vast lands of the Bourbon appanage in central-southern France
– key, therefore, to the king's hopes of military success in Italy.
One of the pageants presented at the entry showed a figure of
Bourbon standing on the back of a stag, his sword as Constable
born upright. The stag pulled a boat – the ship of state, or Francis's
monarchy – along the Rhône. At the stern stood a figure represent-
ing Marshal Trivulzio.[24] Nor were the city's boasts empty. While
in Lyon, Francis secured loans for some 300,000 crowns from
its bankers, and appointed his mother regent of France.[25] He then
gathered his forces at Grenoble, where he was joined by more
than a dozen of the great princes of France, including his uncle

René de Savoie (1473–1525) and his brother-in-law the duc d'Alençon.

On learning of these preparations, the Swiss, hired by Massimiliano Sforza to defend Milan, had immediately secured all the recognized passes through the Alps. Francis made a strategic feint, giving it out that he would probably cross through the pass of Montgenèvre, while actually reconnoitring and clearing a much narrower pass, then called the Col de Larche or l'Argentière, now the Maddalena Pass, which leads into the plain of Piedmont near the town of Cuneo. Sappers cleared and repaired this fairly dangerous route, and the bulk of the army took several days of careful effort to cross it, emerging on the Italian side and marching northeast to Turin. Even as it did so, a small force led by Charles du Solier (1480–1552) and Pierre de Terrail, Chevalier de Bayard (c. 1476–1524), one of France's most renowned soldiers, captured a force of some seven hundred to eight hundred cavalry under the *condottiere* and papal commander Prospero Colonna (1452–1523), which was garrisoned in Villanova. They had been intended to support the Swiss in opposing the French advance, so their capture was a real coup for Francis.[26] Arriving at Turin, the French king opened negotiations with the Swiss, represented by Cardinal Matthäus Schinner (c. 1465–1522) of Sitten, or Sion. Hoping to capitalize on the seizure of their cavalry support, Francis offered them 10 million crowns to evacuate the city and duchy of Milan. The talks made progress at first, so, leaving them in the hands of his delegates, Francis pressed on towards Milan. He crossed the Ticino river, aiming for Lodi, where he hoped to meet the Venetian commander Bartolomeo d'Alviano (1455–1515), whose army was to support the French if needed.

By 10 September an agreement had apparently been reached with the Swiss, and Francis expected a peaceful transition to power in Milan, as had happened for Louis in 1499. In fact, while a minority of the Swiss cantons decided to accept the French offer and withdrew their troops, the majority rejected the deal without, of course, communicating that to Francis. On 13 September the Swiss troops – which liked if possible to attack their enemy before he was ready – urged on by Cardinal Schinner, decided to attack the French camp that afternoon and marched out of Milan towards Lodi.

Francis had established his position southeast of Milan and a little north of Marignano (present-day Melegnano, now part of outer suburban Milan), on the road to Lodi. To the southwest beyond Marignano was Pavia, a strategic stronghold to which Francis could retreat if necessary. He oversaw the final preparation of his position, with his army drawn up in three divisions, each composed of cavalry, infantry and elements of the artillery. On the right was the vanguard, facing Milan to the northwest, commanded by Bourbon and Trivulzio. Some of the artillery (about thirty guns) were placed in a trench line about 30 metres (98 ft) long, protected in front by several ditches and a stream. To the rear of the guns were 10,000 French infantrymen and *Landsknechts* in several blocks, armed with pikes and some *arquebuses*, and about 950 men-at-arms. The main part of the army was at the centre, slightly to the left of and behind the vanguard. Francis commanded the main force of the *gendarmerie*. In front of him were about two-thirds of the heavy guns, and behind them were 17,000 *Landsknechts*, including the 'Black Band' of Guelders. The rearguard was to the king's left, near Santa Brera farm, under Alençon, and comprised more contingents of infantry and the remainder of the guns protected by cavalry.

As usual, the Swiss aimed to hit the French vanguard with as much force as possible in the hope of overwhelming the guns, capturing them and turning them on their opponents. This shock tactic had worked often before, and had made their fearsome reputation as supreme battlefield infantry troops. As they attacked, the Swiss spearhead force, known as a 'forlorn hope', reached the

French artillery. The bishop and chronicler Paolo Giovio (1483–1552) described this force as:

> Elite soldiers chosen among all the Cantons, young and of exceptional physical prowess ... They willingly perform the harshest and most difficult duties of war and usually walk to their death and are praised for that. Because of their astounding fortitude, they are called 'the lost' and are highly esteemed and honoured. Thanks to their virtues, they are allowed to bear the banner and to be infantry captains, and are paid double as long as they live.[27]

And so it proved at Marignano. The block of *Landsknechts* moved forwards to counter the initial Swiss attack. The French cannoneers fired into the ranks of the oncoming Swiss as best they could, but their opponents did capture some French guns. Bourbon led a cavalry charge from the French right in support, against the left flank of the oncoming first Swiss square that followed the spearhead, but it was only partially successful and he fell back with a number of nobles killed or injured. The second Swiss square then moved forwards to support the first, and as dusk fell on a moonlit night, the fighting continued. The main French infantry, including the Black Band, moved forwards, and many cavalry charges were led by the king and Bourbon. The duc de Lorraine was unhorsed but was rescued by Bayard and they made their way back to the French line. The Swiss were checked at the ditch before the artillery, but could not be forced to retreat. At about midnight the moon disappeared behind cloud and the two armies broke apart.[28]

Francis used the early hours of the morning of 14 September to regroup. He sent urgent word to Alviano to bring the Venetians as soon as possible. The guns were better arranged in a wide, shallow arc before the enemy, and their protective earthworks were strengthened. The Swiss, too, regrouped into echelons in shallow steps alongside each other, rather than in sequential squares. At dawn they attacked in this formation along the whole French line. As on the previous day, the French vanguard was on the right, the main 'battle' at the centre and the rearguard on the left. The central square of the Swiss crossed the ditch once more to attack the French guns, but was unsuccessful. The guns were able to keep up frontal and flanking fire on them. Although, as on the previous afternoon, the Swiss forced the French infantry back, Francis counter-attacked with a cavalry charge in support of the central *Landsknechts*, who held their ground. On the right, Bourbon's cavalry charges also had some success against the opposing echelon, but the French left flank looked likely to collapse. Just as it seemed about to do so, and in the best romantic tradition of chivalric warfare, Alviano's Venetian mounted troops arrived under the banner of the Lion of St Mark. They went in to support the French left flank, which held. By now it was mid-morning

Maître à la Ratière, *Battle of Marignan, c.* 1515, illumination on parchment.

and, reinforced and revived, the whole French line launched a massive counter-assault. This time, finally, the Swiss echelons collapsed; they fell back towards Milan, were pursued by the cavalry and the lighter guns, and were routed.

Marignano was a hard battle, fought on a huge scale and estimates of its toll on both sides are difficult because numbers given in contemporary sources vary widely. The Swiss admitted to have lost 5,000 but this seems a major underestimation. Their total deaths and injuries were more likely to have been between 16,000 and 20,000 men. French casualties were perhaps closer to 8,000, including a number of the princes who had flocked to the royal banner. The French king reportedly retired to his tent immediately when he knew he had won, to give thanks for the victory before a crucifix containing a piece of the true Cross. As Alviano saw for himself, Francis, with the support and advice of his experienced marshals, had commanded his army with determination and daring, and had fought personally with real courage in the press of his enemies. This fact was recognized when Chevalier de Bayard accepted the king's request to knight him on the field after the battle.[29]

The importance of coordinated artillery, small arms, infantry and cavalry in warfare was established at Marignano, and the Swiss never regained their reputation as an invincible infantry force. The whole of Europe was brought to the feet of the king of France, who had only just turned 21 while on campaign. He made his formal entry into the city of Milan on 11 October 1515, and seemed – at that moment at least – a new Alexander the Great. This was exactly how the victory was presented in France. For the king himself, Demoulins wrote a three-volume work, *Les Commentaires de la guerre gallique*, in which Francis was represented as the protégé and successor of Julius Caesar, who had written his commentaries on his conquest of Gaul. The volumes imagine a series of flattering dialogues between them as Francis hunts, and in which they discuss warfare and government. They are richly illustrated with miniatures of these encounters. Francis's generals at Marignano were also featured in antique, enamelled roundels attributed to Godefroy le Batave (*fl.* 1516–26) and Jean Clouet (1475?–1540/41).[30]

Francis spent the remainder of the year in and around Milan and Lombardy, imposing his authority on its people and receiving the plaudits of the considerable number of Italian noblemen who came to his court. Sforza went into voluntary exile in France. Francis came to peace terms with ten of the Swiss cantons, in the hope of using their troops in the future. In December he went to Bologna to meet Pope Leo X, who, anxious to protect and enhance his Medici family's interests, recognized Francis as duke of Milan. In return, among other gestures, Francis ennobled the pope's brother Giuliano as duc de Nemours and agreed to begin discussions on a Concordat intended by the pope to overturn the Pragmatic Sanction of Bourges of 1438, which had (theoretically at least) limited papal authority over the Church in France.

Francis returned to his kingdom in January 1516. After receiving news of Marignano, Louise de Savoie and Queen Claude had made their way south, visiting various pilgrimage sites of female saints who had been close to Christ, including that of St Mary Magdalene at Saint-Maximin-la-Sainte-Baume, where the reputed skull of the saint could be found. Francis met them at Sisteron and they made their way together to Marseilles, where Francis and Claude each made a separate formal entry. He was greeted as a returning conquering hero. Here, Francis may also have met his infant daughter, Louise, for the first time. Named after her grandmother, the princess had been born at Amboise on 19 August, as her father crossed the Alps. During the spring, the royal party made its way back north via Lyon to the Loire Valley, where the court remained for the summer. By then, the queen was already pregnant again. In late September, Francis was

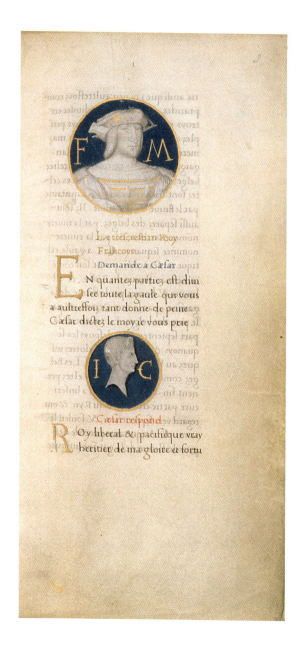

Francis pictured in a medallion above Julius Caesar,
from *Les Commentaires de la guerre gallique*, vol. 1 (1519).

in Paris for the start of the legal year, but the birth at Amboise on 23 October 1516 of his second child, Charlotte, brought him back to the Loire.[31]

The court returned to Paris in the spring of 1517, partly for Queen Claude's coronation, which took place at Saint-Denis on 10 May. It had been postponed twice on account of the queen's pregnancies, and she was soon pregnant again thereafter. Claude made her formal entry into the capital, greeted with elaborate and colourful pageants celebrating women of the Old Testament and other exemplars of female virtue.[32] She was a patron of artists and writers in her own right. Like that of her mother, Anne, Claude's court had a high reputation as a form of finishing school for the daughters of noble houses in France and beyond. We have already noted the presence there for a time from 1519 of Anne Boleyn.

The marriage of Francis and Claude is generally regarded as one of genial, if slightly formal, contentment, and she was a good companion to her husband. At the time of their betrothal, commanded by Louis XII, neither of the young spouses, nor their mothers, had really wanted the union.[33] Yet the queen's steady succession of pregnancies is evidence of her husband's attentions to her, just as it emphasizes the essentially dynastic nature of the royal marriage. Of her, the sixteenth-century commentator Pierre de Bourdeille, seigneur de Brantôme (1540–1614), opined that she 'was very good and very charitable, and very sweet to everyone and never showed displeasure to anybody in her court or of her domains'. He also noted that she was duchess of both Brittany and Milan in right of her mother and father and for the benefit of her husband, 'both duchies joined in all good deed to our beautiful kingdom'. During her frequent confinements, Francis enjoyed the company of other women, but he was hardly unique among kings in that respect. It was not too long into his reign that his 'petite bande' of ladies was known to ambassadors and other observers. Brantôme even alleged that in consequence of these liaisons, Francis had infected his wife with venereal disease, but this cannot be proved.[34]

The court began to grow during these years, rapidly becoming the most glamorous in Europe and attracting quite a large number of Italian artisans, intellectuals and nobles. The most famous was of course Leonardo da Vinci (1452–1519), who arrived in France some time in 1516. Francis gave him the manor house of Cloux at Amboise, and would visit him there when in residence at the royal château. The great man – who was already ailing with paralysis in his right hand – may have done some drawings or other work for the king, but if he did, no direct evidence survives. He died at Cloux in 1519, but not in Francis's arms, as artists and the historian Giorgio Vasari (1511–1574) would later claim, and as is still popularly believed. Francis was at Saint-Germain-en-Laye at the time.

A much younger Italian visitor to the court was Federico Gonzaga (1500–1540), the son of Francesco II Gonzaga, Marquis of Mantua (1466–1519), and Isabella d'Este (1474–1539). Then in his mid-teens, Federico corresponded with his parents – themselves renowned artistic patrons – and the letters are rich with detail about court personalities and entertainments during these opening years of Francis's reign. Between them, Federico and his secretary Stazio Gadio described the events in Bologna in December 1515, Francis's entry into Marseilles the following month and his pilgrimage in May 1516 to the Holy Shroud at Chambéry (now known as the Shroud of Turin), which his mother's family had acquired in 1453.[35] They also made the first contemporary reference to the appearance at court that year of Françoise de Foix, comtesse de Châteaubriant (c. 1495–1537), the sister of Odet, Marshal Lautrec. She had first been a *demoiselle* to Queen Anne, who had arranged and financed her marriage in 1508 to Jean de Laval, comte de Châteaubriant (c. 1490?–1543). Françoise had a

53.

Françoise de Foix, sœur du m.ᵈ de L'autrec et femme de Jean de Laval seign. de Chateaubriant, mort en 1542.

MADAME·DE·CHASTEAVBRIAN

Anonymous, *Françoise de Foix, Comtesse de Châteaubriant*, 1530–37, red chalk and pencil.

daughter, Anne, by him when she was only thirteen. Since then her relationship with her husband had become at least somewhat estranged, and there was talk of what would today be thought of as domestic abuse. Françoise was dark-haired, beautiful, quick-witted and something of a poet herself, and from 1516 Francis courted her assiduously. Federico Gonzaga first met her in June that year. He, too, was charmed by her, especially when she asked him to convey her compliments to his parents. The following month she appeared at a banquet and masque as one of twelve *demoiselles* of Queen Claude, perhaps alongside Anne Boleyn. From 1518 she was also attendant on the princesses of France, implying a closeness to the king.[36]

Poetry was clearly a subject that interested Francis. Whether he was as captivated by music is rather less clear. He was certainly not a musician himself, as was Henry VIII (who was also a composer of some talent). To an extent, his musical patronage perhaps reflected the court's needs more than his own. The chapel royal was the primary musical establishment, with 28 clerks and boy choristers, who could be supplemented with further singers for major events, such as at the Field of Cloth of Gold in 1520. It became known during Francis's reign as 'la chapelle de musique' to distinguish it from the separate 'plainchant' chapel, which the king created. The two most famous musicians who worked in it were Jean Mouton (*c.* 1459–1522), who is likely to have accompanied the king on campaign in 1515, and Claude (or Claudin) de Sermisy (*c.* 1490–1562), who was head of the chapel in the 1520s. The king also had the musicians of the *écurie du roi* (the king's stable), who played trumpets, drums and fifes and provided music for royal entries to cities, outdoor court ceremonial, warfare (on occasion) and the hunt. The king also had a group of musicians for entertainment in the *chambre* and for indoor court entertainments generally, such as the lutenists François Bugats and the Mantuan-born Albert de Rippe, who were initially appointed *valets de chambre* and later *gens de metier*. The French court's musical establishment maintained influential contacts with its counterparts in the Netherlands and Italian courts throughout the king's reign.[37]

Francis and Claude went on a royal tour of Picardy and Normandy in the late summer and autumn of 1517. They were the guests of, among others, Marguerite d'Alençon. In October, during the visit, Francis made his sister duc(hesse) de Berry in her own right, elevating her to the peerage and entitling her to advise him as a counsellor. Louis XII had created his first wife, Jeanne de France, duc de Berry as compensation for her agreement to annul their marriage. At her death in 1505 the duchy had escheated to the crown, and now Francis gave it to his sister, the second of five women to hold it. Such independent status perhaps rewarded Marguerite for her marriage to the intellectually pedestrian Alençon, and acknowledged her support for her younger brother since their childhood.[38] The king spent time hunting there, and Madame de Châteaubriant is likely to have been a member of his small entourage during that trip. She soon became the king's first acknowledged mistress.

As autumn turned to winter, Claude's pregnancy entered its last stages and the court returned to Amboise for her confinement. She and Francis had been praying for an heir since the accession and her first pregnancy in 1515, and the queen's varied pilgrimages in the south later that year and in early 1516 had sustained her hopes. Pleased as they were with their two daughters, the royal couple were mightily relieved when Claude gave birth, on 28 February 1518, to a boy, the dauphin François. In a sense his arrival completed the opening phase of his father's reign, and he was baptised with public triumph and celebration at Easter that year, with Pope Leo as godfather. The prince was given his own household and before he reached his first birthday was himself betrothed in marriage.

The promise Francis had made to the pope to lead a crusade against the Ottomans now fell due. The several years after Marignano were comparatively peaceful in western Europe, but not so in Central Asia and the Middle East. Sultan Bâyezîd II (1447/8–1512) had modernized the Ottoman army and navy. He was succeeded by his son Selîm I (1470–1520), the 'Grim' or 'Resolute', who moved immediately against the Safavid overlord of Persia, Shah Ismail I (1487–1524), advancing into his domain as far south as Tabriz, the capital. Selîm then turned towards Syria and Mamluk Egypt. He took Aleppo in August 1516, followed in quick succession by Damascus and Jerusalem. Syria and Egypt now recognized Selîm's authority, which heralded Ottoman suzerainty over much of the Middle East and North Africa during the reign of his successor, Süleyman. Selîm also made advances into the Balkans, provoking alarm in the West.[39] Leo X wanted a unified response from Christendom's leaders, and this aim had been at least part of his thinking when he accepted Francis's conquest of Milan.

Before Francis could even contemplate, however vaguely, the prospect of leading the fight against Selîm, he needed to secure his position in Europe and to come to terms with the man who was already his greatest rival and threat, Charles of Habsburg. Shortly after his return to France, the king had received word that Ferdinand of Aragon had died, in January 1516. As the heir to Philip, Ferdinand's son-in-law (who had died in 1506), Charles inherited Aragon directly from his grandfather. He also inherited Ferdinand's claim to the kingdom of Naples. Charles also ruled in Castile as regent for his mother, Juana, who had inherited that kingdom from her mother, Isabella, in 1504, but had suffered some form of mental breakdown in the aftermath of her husband's death. The new king needed to go to Spain to claim his inheritances there, and on 13 August 1516 Charles signed the Treaty of Noyon with Francis, a pact intended to secure his interests in the Low

Countries. Charles accepted betrothal to Francis's infant daughter Louise as a substitute for the king's sister-in-law Renée, and Francis promised to recognize Charles's claim to the kingdom of Naples, as Louise's dowry. This also implied that Charles recognized Francis's claim as the successor of the Angevin monarchs before him. He also agreed to an annual tribute of 100,000 crowns for Naples.[40] This was followed in March 1517 by a tripartite alliance incorporating Charles's paternal grandfather, Maximilian. Charles arrived in Spain on 20 September 1517 and remained there for nearly three years attempting to establish his authority in his varied Iberian dominions. Meanwhile, in November 1516 Francis had reached an agreement with the Swiss, known as the Perpetual Peace of Fribourg, that enabled him, in exchange for an enormous sum of 700,000 crowns, to have a near monopoly on hiring mercenaries in the future. The alliance lasted for the remainder of the *ancien régime* and was broken only when the French Revolutionary government invaded Switzerland in 1798. Francis also renewed the important alliance with Venice.

TO RULE AS WELL AS TO REIGN

For the time being, therefore, Francis was at peace, and he probably intended to stay that way as he consolidated his regime at home and built on the personal esteem he enjoyed among his nobles. From the outset, Francis was a monarch with a very strong sense of his own personal and constitutional authority. The financial and legal administration of his diverse kingdom acquired greater complexity and more officials under Francis than ever before, although it was still rudimentary by modern standards. At its head stood the chancellor, Antoine Duprat, who held the Great Seal of the realm and was responsible for recording and giving effect to royal orders through the Chancery. He was assisted by a number of secretaries and notaries. The chancellor also had a number of deputies, the *maîtres des requêtes d'hôtel*, whose wide-ranging judicial and administrative functions mirrored his, and made them principal royal agents and representatives. The chancellor supervised the operation of the sovereign courts of the kingdom and the judiciary generally. The highest legal court was the *Grand Conseil*, which exercised a supervisory jurisdiction over all the other courts, resolving conflicts between laws and acting as a court of appeal. It still travelled with the king but should be distinguished from his personal advisory body the *conseil du roi*, which itself had an outer group and, under Francis, also an inner, narrow circle of no more than three or four councillors, the *conseil étroit*. Almost as high as the *Grand Conseil* (certainly in its own estimation) was the *Parlement* of Paris. It was a sovereign court with a wide-ranging original jurisdiction in matters involving the king's person and interests, and also had an appellate jurisdiction. By the time of Francis's reign there were also six provincial *parlements*. They fulfilled the important function of reviewing and registering royal ordinances to give them legal effect in France, after satisfying themselves that such ordinances complied with the 'fundamental laws' of the country, a form of unwritten constitution whereby kings were held accountable for their exercise of power.

Royal power in the localities was held primarily by a group of noblemen appointed as provincial governors, each a form of lieutenant-general, who exercised a wide range of military, legal and administrative powers and answered to the king and chancellor directly. The prestige of the governors was already increasing before Francis's reign. They helped to ensure royal authority was obeyed, and coordinated activity with the provincial *parlements* or estates. Although primarily intended to supervise, they could also exercise a representative role for provincial elites on significant concerns, most usually defence and taxation. The governors were assisted by officials, the *baillis* and *sénéchaux*, whose functions were mainly judicial. Major governors were nearly always also commanders of ordinance companies, so had close connections with the noble families of their provinces. As such, they acted as crown patrons in these localities, brokering military, civil and royal court appointments. They kept the king in touch with those upon whose support he depended, and upon whose service and loyalty he could rely.[41]

Claude de Seyssel (*c.* 1450–1520), a Savoyard lawyer and *parlementaire*, wrote *La Monarchie de France* in the spring of 1515, dedicating it to the new king. His work was both a defence and an explanation of the unwritten French constitution, which, he argued, supported and enabled the kings of France to rule effectively. Seyssel affirmed the final authority of the king but also insisted that there were certain agreed restraints or 'freins' upon his power. French constitutional theory recognized a distinction between tyranny and the exercise of legitimate kingship. Contrary to the views of contemporary English propagandists, the French king could not simply do whatever he liked. In all his decisions, Francis was expected to act in accordance with Christian values and with the advice of his council and judges. His royal legitimacy and authority were recognized on that basis. If the *Parlement* of Paris found the king to be acting beyond his powers, it could refuse to register a royal ordinance. It could also issue a formal *remonstrance*, to which the king was obliged to respond. He could ultimately enforce his authority through a formal process, the *lit de justice*, whereby, in person, he insisted upon the registration of his ordinances by the *Parlement*. Such occasions were, however, very rare.[42]

These were matters of interpretation, and Francis always insisted publicly that his authority should be obeyed without question. The sovereign courts were equally insistent on their right to scrutinize his edicts. Each side vigorously tested the limits of, and pushed at, the boundaries of royal power. In practice, therefore, Francis had to negotiate and have his decisions examined, but ultimately he retained full sovereignty and his alone was the final decision in any matter before him. This somewhat paradoxical principle was summarized in the phrase *la monarchie absolue*, which meant that the king had 'final authority'. It should not in any circumstance be confused with the derivative English term 'absolute monarchy', at least as it is commonly misunderstood: to mean untrammelled royal power. The king of France had wide executive power, but he could not act as a tyrant.

Exactly these issues arose in several controversies after the king's return to France in 1516. The most significant of them was over the Concordat of Bologna, agreed in principle in December 1515, when Francis and Leo X had met in that northern Italian city, and approved by Leo in August 1516. In a very technical way, it recognized the pope's right to make appointments to senior ecclesiastical benefices. The problem was that there was a legal tradition in France, dating back to at least the fourteenth century if not well before, that the king was 'emperor in his kingdom' and not subject to any other authority in the realm, including the papacy. Ecclesiastical institutions within France were answerable primarily to the king, before the pope. This tradition, known as Gallicanism, had received legislative force in the Pragmatic Sanction of Bourges of 1438, which had limited papal power in France by prescribing that, theoretically at least, all episcopal and abbatial appointments in the Church were to be by election. The pope's role was simply to confirm the elected candidates. It also abolished annual payments (annates) to the papacy. It apparently gave greater control over appointments to the Church itself, freeing it from papal interference. Since that time, successive popes had urged its abrogation.

In fact, elections to important ecclesiastical office in France were constantly subject to royal and noble interference, especially given the frequent disputes over candidates for particularly high-status benefices. The Concordat recognized limits of age and qualification upon candidates for senior benefices, and under its terms the papacy again 'instituted' or formally made the appointment to a benefice. The Concordat thus apparently curtailed the Pragmatic Sanction, as Leo intended that it should. The realm's highest judicial body, the *Parlement* of Paris, certainly took that view and refused to register the agreement, on the grounds that the Concordat infringed French sovereignty and that this was against the unwritten constitution. The Faculty of Theology at the University of Paris endorsed the *Parlement*'s position. The Sorbonne was concerned to maintain the privileged access enjoyed by its graduates to some of the best sinecures, under its influence.

Appearances were, however, deceptive. If anything, the Concordat actually increased crown, not papal, control over appointments, while technically conceding their formalization to the papacy. For Francis, the Concordat was the price of the pope's recognition of him as duke of Milan, and he was furious because, for him, the *Parlement*'s refusal to ratify the Concordat was not just politically inconvenient, given the alliance it secured with the pope, but a challenge to his royal and personal authority. As Chancellor Duprat insisted, the Concordat in fact maintained the freedom of the French Church from Rome, under crown protection and authority. The courts and university should be grateful for that, not otherwise. They, however, were not sure that one master was better than any other. It took a long campaign of persuasion, insistence and even intimidation by Francis and royal officials before the *Parlement* finally registered the Concordat, still under protest, on 22 March 1518.[43]

By that time, Leo, hoping to capitalize on the comparative calm in western Europe, had called for a formal truce between its leaders in order to plan united action against the Ottomans. To this, Henry of England had made a ready response. He had reportedly been close to tears when the scale and style of Francis's victory at Marignano had been confirmed in the autumn of 1515.

Since then he had promoted several schemes with the papacy for action against the French in Milan, including his own renewed alliance with Maximilian and Charles in 1517, but none of these posed any immediate threat to Francis. It was Cardinal Wolsey who, early in the spring of 1518, proposed, instead of a papal truce, a multilateral non-aggression pact that banned war permanently between all signatories and promised collective action against any one state that broke the agreement. It was, first and foremost, an effort to curb Francis and to catapult Henry back to centre stage through his sponsorship of the first European collective security agreement – a forerunner of NATO. The ancient ideal of peace throughout Christendom brought about by rulers acting in concert was given new effect in the second Treaty of London, signed in October 1518, which was also known as the Treaty of Universal Peace. The linchpin of the new peace was to be an Anglo-French alliance, secured by the betrothal of Henry's daughter Mary (born in February 1516) to the dauphin François, two years her junior.[44]

Wolsey's dramatic intervention presented something of a dilemma for Francis. Despite the idealistic and somewhat abstract rhetoric with which it was promulgated, peace-making between late medieval monarchs was never done for its own sake. For Francis, as for his counterparts elsewhere, peace had always to be 'with honour' or advantage. Wolsey understood that perfectly well. Knowing that Francis still wanted Tournai back, he now offered it, at a substantial price, as an inducement to join the treaty. Getting Tournai back would certainly be welcome, but a non-aggression pact had potentially serious implications for Francis's hold on Milan and Lombardy. On the one hand, it would be useful in constraining Maximilian and Charles from threatening his grasp on the duchy, but on the other he might be prevented from taking military action there himself. Moreover, his ducal title had been recognized by Pope Leo, who now wanted him to join the peace. Francis had already promised Leo that he would lead action against the Ottomans once he had secured the succession. In the summer of that year, Leo gave Francis a painting commissioned from Raphael, *St Michael Vanquishing Satan*. St Michael (Saint-Michel) was the patron of the French order of chivalry, founded by Louis XI in 1469, and the insignia of the order bore the image of the saint. By the time of Francis's reign, St Michael had become a representation of the French king himself, so that the gift was very likely to have been intended to remind Francis not only of his Concordat with the papacy, but of his personal promise to Leo to lead a crusade.[45]

Membership of a Christian league might also be very useful in such an enterprise if it came to it, and Francis had already begun negotiations with the Electors of the German empire about the possibility of his succeeding the ailing Maximilian as Holy Roman Emperor. Henry's support and that of Leo in such an effort might be helpful and would be more easily demanded if Francis had co-operated with Wolsey's scheme. In light of these considerations, Francis therefore accepted the alliance on offer from Henry. He agreed to pay 600,000 crowns for Tournai and to renew the annual subsidy payments Louis had undertaken. Henry was also to hold a group of young French courtiers hostage as a guarantee that Francis would perform his obligations under the treaty.[46]

A large French embassy, led by Admiral Bonnivet, one of the heroes of Marignano, was sent to London in September 1518 for the signing of the Treaty of London. Its members were treated with conspicuous generosity and favour by Henry and the whole English court, as an expression of the king's apparent esteem for Francis. The treaty was sworn to at St Paul's Cathedral on 3 October, during a Mass celebrated by Wolsey with all possible solemnity. Richard Pace, one of the king's secretaries, delivered an oration that apparently praised peace in a way that Erasmus would have endorsed but which, reading between the lines, was really a warning to the French against infringing the terms of the

Raphael, *St Michael Vanquishing Satan*, 1518, oil on canvas, transferred from wood.

treaty; it also praised Henry's potential as the leader of Christendom.
A reciprocal English embassy was received in Paris in December
and was accorded every courtesy by Francis and his court. Entertainments included a splendid banquet held at the Bastille on
the night of the winter solstice, at which Francis made a dramatic
entrance before the English ambassadors as the 'Sun' king who
banished the darkness of conflict and brought the light by which
Christendom would find its way against the Ottomans. It was
intended to show, in other words, that his participation in the
Treaty of London showed that *he* was the real leader of Christendom,
upon whom Henry, Wolsey and indeed Pope Leo depended, if
the Universal Peace were to be successful.[47]

Under the terms of the treaty, Henry and Francis were due
to meet personally in 1519 to affirm their alliance, but the death
of Emperor Maximilian in January that year caused a postpone-
ment as both monarchs competed with Charles of Spain to succeed
him. Francis had the better chance, limited though it always was,
and expected Henry's support in return for that which he had
given the Universal Peace. This delicate situation required considerable diplomatic skill from England's first resident ambassador
in France, Sir Thomas Boleyn (father of a famous daughter), who
was appointed to his post late in 1518. One welcome opportunity to engender good relations came with the birth of Francis's
second son, Henri, in March 1519. He was apparently named after
Henry of England, who became his godfather. At Henri's baptism
in June, Sir Thomas presented the child with gifts from the king
of England. Charles of Spain also expected Henry's support, but
it was his money that finally told when the ballot of the imperial
electors was held in June. Henry was entertaining some of the
French hostages at Penshurst Place in Kent when he received
the news of Charles's election as 'King of the Romans', the first
stage in the process of his becoming Holy Roman Emperor. The
Venetian ambassador in England noted that Henry was careful to

pretend to them 'that he greatly regretted that King Francis had not been elected'.[48]

Francis was as keen as Henry to move on after the imperial election. Plans were therefore agreed early in 1520 for a meeting in the Pas-de-Calais, between the English town of Guînes and the French town of Ardres. The event became known as the Field of Cloth of Gold. It was essentially a tournament jointly hosted by the two kings to inaugurate the Universal Peace. Tournaments were the conventional way for medieval elites to celebrate the making of peace and friendship. In that sense it was literally a war game, but one the rules and stratagems of which had important implications for Francis and his role in Europe. Like Henry, Francis spent lavishly on the event and each monarch brought some 5,000–6,000 noblemen and -women to the Field with him. The members of the French entourage were accommodated in Ardres, in the villages about, and in a multitude of tents and pavilions erected in the fields beneath the town. On Francis's orders, issued in February 1520, the materials for making and dressing the tents were prepared in Tours, an important cloth town. More than four hundred packhorses then brought the canvas and timber needed for the tents up from the Loire Valley to Ardres. Once erected, the pavilions were covered with hundreds of yards of blue, violet and crimson velour, velvet, silk and the cloth of gold that gave the event its name. Francis also had some kind of *hôtel particulier* specially constructed for him in Ardres. It may have been designed by the Italian architect Domenico da Cortona.[49] Francis began his journey to Ardres in the Loire Valley, where he had begun the year. He came up to Paris, gathering elements of his entourage there and along the rest of the way. He arrived at Ardres on the appointed date of Thursday, 31 May. Queen Claude accompanied her husband despite being heavily pregnant with her fifth child, since her presence as the pre-eminent French hostess to the English court was vital. She was assisted in that role by Louise de Savoie and Marguerite d'Alençon.[50]

Francis first met Henry in the early evening of Thursday, 7 June. The moment is depicted in a series of bas-reliefs from the 1530s in the courtyard of the Hôtel de Bourgtheroulde in Rouen, Normandy. The pair are shown on horseback, about to embrace, Henry on the left and Francis on the right. The tournament began on 11 June and continued for about ten days. Henry and Francis, as apparent brothers-in-arms, led mixed teams of French and English knights as the challengers for the tournament. They fought similarly constituted teams of responders. The tournament comprised three competitions: jousting, mounted combat in the arena between groups of knights, and foot combat over barriers. Like Henry, Francis wore a succession of spectacularly colourful and allegorical costumes. Over the four days on which he jousted, his dress spelled out, on little books made of silk and chained to one another, the phrase 'heart fastened in pain end-less/ when she/ delivereth me/ not of bonds'. Like his salamander emblem, the message of these and other decorative costumes was that Francis had a passionate nature impelled by chivalric love, but was also a monarch educated in moral philosophy and the highest principles of governance.[51]

Francis and his leading courtiers were entertained on three occasions over the fortnight by Queen Katherine and the English court, while Henry was entertained at Ardres by the French queen's household. Each side strove to outdo the other in the number and variety of courses, their culinary ingenuity and the panache with which they were served. On one occasion, however, Francis demanded very particular hospitality when he made an extraordinary impromptu visit to Henry, of which the seigneur de Florange left an account. On the morning of Sunday, 17 June he rose early at Ardres and rode to Guînes castle, accompanied by only a few close courtiers. On arrival, he demanded to be taken to Henry's private apartments. Francis first banged on the door, then entered the English king's chamber unannounced. To a surprised Henry,

who was not long out of bed, Francis grandly declared himself a prisoner while assuring him of his good faith. He then helped Henry on with his shirt. They embraced and Henry gave Francis a collar of great value. Francis responded by giving Henry his own collar or jewelled bracelets (the sources vary). Henry then took Francis to meet Katherine and her ladies, with whom the French king stayed until later in the day, when the rest of his close household arrived for a banquet hosted by the queen of England.

Historians have been sceptical about the story, but Florange insisted in his account that Francis had panicked his own court by the action, and it had been at his own initiative.[52] Whether entirely spontaneous or not, it played upon the recent traditions of Anglo-French relations and on more remote traditions of medieval diplomacy and the law of arms, and it was replete with paradox and double meaning. Calling himself a prisoner, actually a hostage, to Henry was an apparent demonstration of his own good faith. It was, simultaneously, a considerable imposition on Henry, who became responsible for the protection and honourable treatment of Francis while the French ruler was with him — an extraordinarily provocative gesture. Helping to dress the English

British school, *The Field of the Cloth of Gold*, *c.* 1545, oil on canvas.

king, although apparently an act of great humility in Francis, was
also a bold assertion of his right as one sovereign to behave famil-
iarly towards another. Henry wanted Francis to accept that getting
what he wanted depended on keeping the terms of the agreements
they were making. Francis knew that, but with the visit to Guînes
he sought to personalize peace between himself and Henry. He
seems to have wanted to upset the delicate balance of protocol
at the event, and his visit was intended both to impress and
intimidate.

Whether in the longer term the gesture worked quite as well
as Francis hoped is doubtful, but it paid off handsomely in the
short term, and it offers an insight into his personality and manner
of dealing with people. The Mantuan ambassador, Soardino,
reported from the Field that two days later, in the early morning,
the English king responded with a somewhat ponderous reciprocal
visit to Ardres. There was a second round of gift exchanges, but
Soardino's report captures neatly the way Francis's gambit had
worked. He observed:

> The whole court of France rejoices, for until now, no mark
> of confidence had been displayed by the English king; nay
> in all matters he invariably evinced small trust; but the Most
> Christian King has *compelled* him to make this demonstra-
> tion, having set the example by placing himself with such
> assurance in his hands last Sunday in the Castle of Guînes.[53]

The Field ended formally with a High Mass celebrated on
23 June by Cardinal Wolsey in a specially made chapel erected at
the tiltyards. The chapels royal of England and France sang alter-
native parts of the Mass, and the kings and queens exchanged
greetings of peace. At or about the moment of the elevation of the
Host, there appeared in the sky above the tiltyard chapel, at the
height of a crossbow bolt shot, what one French description called

'une grande salemandre ou dragon faicte artificiellement' (a large artificially made salamander or dragon). This was evidently a kite made by the English, drawn on a cable from the French town of Ardres towards Guînes and over the chapel. The 'dragon' had blazing eyes and its mouth hissed with smoke, indicating that pyrotechnics of some sort were involved. A fire-breathing salamander decoration had featured at a banquet given at the Bastille in December 1518 for the English ambassadors who had come to ratify the participation of Francis in the Universal Peace. Such imagery was reported back and would have been fresh in the minds of the English court. The device might have been intended to represent Henry's Welsh ancestry, or it may well be that it was, as the French source interpreted it, a royal salamander, flown as a compliment to Francis on the eve of the end of the meeting.

The two kings farewelled each other the following day, exchanging expensive gifts and promises of meeting again. Francis's participation in the Field was his way of saying that Henry could call himself king of France or whatever he liked, but that the English ruler remained dependent on Francis's goodwill and active support if he were to have the kind of significant role in Europe that Wolsey envisaged. If he were now the 'good brother and friend', as they called each other, Francis expected Henry's support in the defence of France and against Charles. Francis proffered friendship as an acknowledgement of *his* own power over France and his importance beyond it. Why else, after all, did Henry first suggest this meeting? For all the sport, the jousting, the banqueting and the gift-giving, the two kings' interaction at the Field of Cloth of Gold was finally about each expressing his own sense of himself and offering peace and friendship to the other, on his own terms.

Unfortunately, despite genuine effort initially, Francis could not repose enough confidence in the Universal Peace to allay his (not unreasonable) fears that it would merely allow Charles V the means to consolidate his power and threaten Milan. The French king therefore took what he saw as a bold gamble: to trigger the collective security mechanism of that peace by launching a covert attack on Charles in the spring of 1521. Far from securing all that he had gained and built on since his accession in 1515, however, this decision very nearly cost him the kingdom of France.

TWO

A Kingdom in the Hazard

To inform you of the extent of my misfortune, of everything, nothing is left but my honour and my life, so that the news of me may in some wise comfort you . . . I beg you not to lose heart but to exercise your accustomed prudence, for I have proved that God will not finally abandon me.[1]

hese words were written by Francis I to his mother in the days after his defeat at the Battle of Pavia in February 1525. A decade into his reign, the king reached his greatest personal crisis. The complete loss of what might fairly be described as a wholly unnecessary war left his kingdom in the greatest danger from its enemies, the like of which had not been experienced since the darkest days of the Hundred Years War. For France to extricate itself from this predicament required not only the skill and diligence of his ministers, chief among whom was Louise, but a great deal of deception and a fair bit of luck.

After the Field of Cloth of Gold, the vast numbers of people who had assembled for the event dispersed quickly whence they had come. Great play of it was soon made publicly in France, with descriptions printed in Paris and on sale on its streets. In England, however, it was forgotten virtually overnight. Francis and his immediate entourage made their way back to Paris. The king

and queen travelled by river down to Amiens, where he inspected
fortifications and ordered new defensive works to be carried out
on the approaches to the city. The royal party arrived back at
Saint-Germain-en-Laye on 10 July and a month later the queen
was delivered of her fifth child, Madeleine.[2]

Charles V had met Henry VIII at Calais immediately after
the Field, but there had been no Anglo-Imperial alliance such as
the emperor (and the pope) had wanted, and that Francis had
feared. Nevertheless, Francis's orders at Amiens perhaps indicate that hopes of a long-lasting peace were not that high. On
23 October Charles was crowned king of the Romans at Aachen
and took the title 'Emperor'. The pope invited him to Rome to
be crowned formally and complete the process of his elevation.
Francis fretted that peace would only weaken his position and
allow Charles to build his power. He was not worried about
France as such, but rather that Charles would threaten his hold
on Milan and Lombardy, and his further claim to the kingdom
of Naples. Francis sent one of his close courtiers, François de Saint-
Marsault, to Leo X in an attempt to secure his agreement not to
allow Charles to threaten Milan, and also to confer the kingdom
of Naples, if not on Francis, then upon Henri d'Orléans, his youngest son. Francis also intended to go personally to Milan to oversee
its defence and to dissuade Charles from any aggressive action
there, but, only a few days into the new year, the king suffered a
near-fatal injury.

The Christmas court revels at the château of Romorantin
concluded on the night of 6 January with a mock siege of the
lodgings of François de Bourbon, comte de Saint-Pol (1491–1545).
In the course of the defenders throwing eggs, stones and suchlike
at the assailants, one of them had the bright idea of dropping a
partially burnt branch or log, taken from a fireplace, from an upper
window. Unfortunately, the king was standing immediately below.
It struck him on the head with such force that it knocked him

senseless. He was in serious danger for some days and it took him several months to recover from the injury, tended all the while by his anxious mother.[3]

This injury prevented Francis from going to Milan as early as he had planned but during his convalescence he received Robert II de La Marck, duc de Bouillon and seigneur de Sedan (1468–1536), the father of his friend Florange. La Marck was then in dispute with the emperor over various lands he held as vassal on the borders of the empire. Soon afterwards, encouraged by a payment of 10,000 crowns from Francis, La Marck left Charles's service and swore allegiance to the French king. He then attacked the emperor's territory in Luxembourg. At the same time, Francis offered covert military support to Henri d'Albret (1503–1555), the French claimant to the kingdom of Navarre, most of which had been taken by Ferdinand of Aragon in 1512–13. This strategic subterfuge of creating distracting conflicts for Charles to have to deal with fooled nobody. As early as April 1521 the imperial ambassador at the French court accused Francis of being behind both these moves, and Charles soon counter-attacked, throwing La Marck out of Luxembourg and advancing to the borders of France. The outcome in Navarre was no more successful. After initially taking the small mountain kingdom, the French commander André de Foix, seigneur de Lesparre (1490–1547), younger brother of Odet and Françoise, overreached himself in Castile and was beaten back out of Navarre altogether. Pope Leo had never been happy with French power in the Italian peninsula, and, seeing the actions of Francis for what they were, in May 1521 he repudiated their recent agreement over Milan. Francis struck back with financial sanctions that only alienated the pope further. Francis's disastrous decision to support La Marck also gave Charles the opportunity he had by then long wanted, to make his own name in chivalric defence of his rights – just as Francis had seen himself doing in 1515. Encouraged by his chancellor, Mercurino di Gattinara (1465–1530), Charles attacked the French city of Tournai and made plans for action in Italy.

Alarmed by the vehemence of the imperial and papal responses to his own covert actions, Francis now tried to play the 'Universal Peace' card, claiming that he was the victim of imperial aggression and calling on England to support him as an ally under the mutual defence terms of the Treaty of London. But Wolsey called his bluff. Instead of immediately assisting Francis as an ally, Henry acted out his role as the 'arbiter' or arbitrator of international affairs. With his usual high-flown rhetoric, Wolsey, as the king's cardinal, convened a conference at Calais in August 1521 to try to resolve the problems. Grand Chancellor Gattinara represented the emperor and Chancellor Antoine Duprat spoke for Francis, but no real dialogue ensued. The French were initially happy to try to use the talks to bring about a truce, but the imperialists were wary lest the fighting season be lost in elaborate quibbling over who was primarily responsible for the outbreak of war. Francis seems initially to have trusted and been guided by Wolsey. Unable to resolve the differences between the parties, however, Wolsey's priority soon became keeping Henry on the winning side in the conflict. He did some covert scheming of his own, negotiating behind the scenes with the emperor at Bruges to conclude a secret treaty that committed Henry to an alliance and a war against Francis in 1523 unless the Franco-Imperial conflict had ended by November 1521. Francis's daughter Charlotte was to be replaced by Henry's daughter Mary as Charles's prospective bride. Since no progress was made at Calais and as Charles's military capacity increased, it was Francis and Louise who became frustrated, especially when Ardres was attacked in September. Both Louise and Marguerite accused Wolsey of treachery in his dealings with France. Francis now resisted calls for a truce, partly encouraged by Bayard's stout defence of Mézières in September. He fought to relieve the imperial siege of his recently repurchased city of Tournai. The weather and his fortunes, however, turned once more and, by the end of November 1521, the city was lost to Charles. This loss was somewhat offset by the Constable's capture of the imperial town of Hesdin the same month, but far worse for Francis was to follow.

The Treaty of Bruges between Henry and Charles, now incorporating Leo X, was formally signed in November. On 19 November imperial and papal troops under Francis's old adversary Prospero Colonna took Milan again, forcing Marshal Lautrec, Francis's commander in Italy, to evacuate the Milanais and retreat to Cremona, although the French garrison in the city held out. Francis called on the Swiss for terms, and some 16,000 Swiss and Venetian troops were soon marching to join Lautrec and his brother Lescun. Leo had finally got the best of Francis, as he had been earnestly seeking to do since Marignano six years earlier. It is doubtful that he knew much about it, however, since he had been ill for some time and he died on 1 December. He was succeeded early the following year by Adrian of Utrecht (1459–1523), Cardinal-Bishop of Tortosa, former tutor to Charles v and, at the time, his regent in Spain. Pope Adrian vi did not arrive in Rome until August 1522. Francis was disappointed at his election, but in fact once in post Adrian proved less a 'creature' of the emperor than the king might first have supposed. He favoured peace and urged a resolution of the Franco-Imperial conflict, and Francis responded positively, on the understanding of course that Milan would be restored to him.

In April 1522 Lautrec and his troops moved towards Milan, but an imperial and papal army under Colonna intervened, attempting to trap the French between itself and Pavia. Seeing the trap, Lautrec retreated to Monza but was pursued by Colonna, who established a fortified camp in the grounds of the villa of La Bicocca, about 6.5 kilometres (4 mi.) north of Milan. Rather as had happened at Marignano in 1515, the impetuous Swiss mercenaries now fighting for, rather than against, France wanted the chance of a pitched battle to win all, and in the hope of booty. Lautrec had virtually no choice but to agree to what he considered a point-less attack, on 27 April. Once more the Swiss charged the enemy's artillery and, as at Marignano, were slaughtered in vast numbers. The result was that they and their French commanders were driven out of Lombardy and Genoa altogether. This was precisely the outcome that Francis's covert war in the spring of 1521 had been intended to anticipate and avoid. He had now lost virtually all that he had won since 1515 by war and by complex, sometimes devious and always expensive diplomacy. But there was perhaps one comforting event for Francis amid all these setbacks. On 22 January 1522 his third son, Charles (1522–1545), was born at Saint-Germain-en-Laye and created duc d'Angoulême.

Meanwhile, another Charles, the emperor, was coming to terms with the consequences of the revolt of the *comuneros* against his rule in Castile and other parts of Spain, which had broken out at about the time he had left for England and Flanders back in May 1520. His nobles had stayed loyal to him and eventually put down the uprising in the towns, but he needed to return to Spain to re-establish his authority. Francis watched as the emperor retraced his steps, leaving the Netherlands and arriving in England on 27 May, there to be greeted with extravagant generosity by Henry, with public celebrations of the Anglo-Imperial alliance agreed the previous autumn. These ceremonies included a formal joint entry to London by Charles and Henry on 6 June, dressed identically to emphasize their apparent equality and unity, almost exactly two years to the day after Henry and Francis had first met, in similar fraternal spirit, near Guînes.[4] Even as the English court entertained its guest, Henry's herald, Clarenceux King of Arms, arrived at Lyon. There, with an imperial herald, on 29 May, he formally 'defied' Francis on behalf of Henry and so declared war. After a month of feasting and hunting with Henry, the

Jean Clouet, *Odet de Foix, Vicomte de Lautrec, c.* 1516, chalk on paper.

emperor embarked from Southampton and arrived in Santander on 16 July 1522.

Appearances were deceptive, however. Henry and Wolsey had insisted during the emperor's visit that a joint Anglo-Imperial attack on France should wait until 1524. Despite ordering some coastal raiding on Brittany and around the Pas-de-Calais pursuant to the alliance, the English king had insufficient money to launch himself against Francis immediately. Wolsey perhaps hoped that delay would lead to a renewed peace. During 1523 Henry turned his attention instead to the Scots, hoping to forestall any Stuart interference in an English campaign against France, should it ever happen. Yet it was a completely unexpected turn of events in France that finally galvanized Henry and Wolsey into action.

In what proved to be the only seriously intended aristocratic revolt of the French king's reign, Charles, duc de Bourbon, planned to renounce his allegiance to Francis. The cause of the Constable's discontent was the status and security of his lands. On 28 April Charles's wife, Suzanne, had died. The daughter of Anne de Beaujeu, niece of Charles VIII and granddaughter of Louis XI, Suzanne had extensive lands. Her marriage to Charles had been intended to preserve the connection between the crown and the vast Bourbon appanage, a mini-kingdom in effect, in southern central France. Having no children when she died, complicated questions of inheritance and of Bourbon's potential next marriage arose. Some of her lands escheated to the crown in the circum-stances; others did not. Francis and his mother, who was Suzanne's cousin and nearest relative at the latter's death, moved to take full advantage of the situation for the crown. There was an initial suggestion that Louise and Bourbon might marry, but since she was older than him and perhaps unlikely to have children, he re-jected this out of hand. Their initial stratagem having failed, Francis and Louise then sought to exploit the legal complexities of the Bourbon inheritance, and complicated lawsuits began. They pre-empted the outcome of these proceedings when, in August 1523, Francis made Louise regent for the second time in his reign as he prepared to fight once more for Milan. Perhaps under her influence, the *Parlement* of Paris ordered the confiscation of Bourbon's lands. Some of this rough-and-ready legal action may have been prompted by the possibility that Bourbon might marry the recently widowed Eleanor of Portugal (1498–1558), also known as Eleanor of Castile (or of Austria), the sister of Charles V. An offer had certainly been made. This only heightened the anxiety in the Valois circle about Bourbon's power and potential if he married into the Habsburgs.[5]

An exasperated and perhaps fearful Bourbon did attract some support from those among his own noble clients who objected to the way the king and his mother were moving. During the summer of 1523 Bourbon began negotiations with Charles V and Henry to assist him financially and to invade France in support of his proposed insurrection, set for August. Then Bourbon hesitated. An unwilling rebel at best, it seems, and under considerable pressure, Bourbon feigned illness when confronted by the king himself at Moulins in August, but promised to follow Francis on campaign to Milan when he had recovered. It looked as if some sort of reconciliation might be on the cards. Yet, in early September, Bourbon met Henry's envoy, Sir John Russell, secretly to discuss the terms and extent of potential English support, although he balked at Russell's insistence that he acknowledge Henry as his rightful sovereign and king of France. Wary of such conditional assistance, Bourbon finally abandoned any idea of a *coup d'état* and fled to imperial territory in Franche-Comté and from there to Turin.

Too late, an English army of some 10,000 troops under the Duke of Suffolk invaded Picardy the same month. Confused English strategic aims saw Suffolk initially trying to capture Boulogne, then being ordered to march rapidly towards Paris to try to link up with the armies supposedly being raised by Charles and

Bourbon. By late October the English army was only 80 kilometres (50 mi.) from Paris and, with the king away in Lyon preparing for his Milan campaign, there was panic in the capital. Ditches were dug, chains slung across the main streets and other defensive measures put in hand. Fortunately for Francis, Lautrec was able to halt the progress of such Spanish troops as did invade France from the southwest and, as we have seen, Bourbon's rising came to nothing. Having no support and with supply lines overstretched, the English army withdrew to Calais as the winter set in. Louise de Savoie began secret peace negotiations with the English, aimed at detaching Henry from his alliance with Charles and dissuading him from a renewed campaign in France.[6] As all this played out, Queen Claude was delivered, on 5 June 1523, of her fourth daughter and her seventh (and last) child, Marguerite (1523–1574), named after her aunt. As a young adult in 1559 the princess would play a vital part in resolving Franco-Habsburg conflict during her brother Henri's reign, under the Treaty of Cateau-Cambrésis.

RETURN TO ITALY: THE BATTLE OF PAVIA

Pope Adrian VI died in September 1523, even as Francis, for the second time since Marignano, sent an army to recover Milan and Lombardy. Its commander, Bonnivet, could do little with winter coming on, however, save blockade the city from a military camp at Abbiategrasso. The accession of Leo X's cousin Cardinal Giulio de' Medici as Pope Clement VII (1478–1534) in November 1523 can hardly have pleased Francis. A second apparently pro-imperial Medici pope would presumably oppose his aims in Milan. Yet, as had Adrian before him, Clement proved more neutral than the king expected. He refused an anti-French alliance with Charles and initiated peace proposals between the enemies. This disappointed Charles, who allowed his new commander, Colonna's successor Charles de Lannoy, viceroy of Naples (c. 1487–1527), to move against Bonnivet. The Admiral was forced to withdraw, and he was wounded in the process, shot by an *arquebusier*. So, too, was the Chevalier Bayard, who, at the age of 48, succumbed to his wounds on 30 April. By the summer the French had been forced back over the Alps once more.[7]

Meanwhile, Bourbon reached a new agreement – or at least thought he had – with Charles and Henry, this time for a tripartite invasion of France. Wolsey had never really been persuaded of Bourbon's intentions or strength, and money was tight following the fruitless invasion of the previous September. Contrary to those expectations, however, Bourbon did raise an army and in July crossed into France from Lombardy, moving west rapidly along the south coast in the hope of linking up with imperial troops to be sent from Spain. He took Aix and went on to besiege Marseilles in August 1524, but the Spanish armies did not arrive to assist him. Thoughts of renewed English support for him briefly revived at the news of his success, but these came to nothing. Francis, who had been in Lyon monitoring events in Lombardy, had returned to the Loire Valley that spring. He now left Blois and an ailing Queen Claude behind him and met up with a recuperated Bonnivet. He brought a royal army of about 6,000 Swiss infantry and the *gendarmerie* down to Avignon by September. Seeing its approach, unable to make progress at Marseilles and facing a rebellion by his own troops, Bourbon hurriedly withdrew along the coast and over the border, allowing Francis to retake Aix. The king now pursued Bourbon as he retreated to Lombardy, determined once more to fight for Milan, despite the lateness in the season, and apparently brimming with confidence. He had, after all, done this before. Louise moved to Saint-Just-sur-Lyon once more to facilitate communications with her son and based what became her second, and most important, regency there. Even as she did so, she pressed her envoy in London to come to an agreement with Wolsey to keep England out of a renewed war. Wolsey made it clear that any agreement would come at a high price, and for the moment they made little progress. Yet Louise's persistence would soon prove crucial to France's interests.

On 17 October 1524 Francis crossed the Alps for the second time, in personal command of an army of about 30,000–40,000 troops (or so he was reported to have told Clement VII) and by a rather easier route than he had taken almost a decade earlier. Rejecting the pope's attempt to mediate, he boasted of having the means to achieve his aims, which were nothing less than the entire duchy of Milan and the kingdom of Naples into the bargain.[8] Swiss mercenary troops were once again on his side, but the *Landsknechts*, under Charles de Lannoy, would prove their equal. With him was Fernando Francesco d'Avalos, Marquis of Pescara (1489/90–1525), who had joined Bourbon's invasion of Provence and retreated with him, pursued by Francis. The king of France was joined by virtually all his principal noblemen and commanders, including the Foix brothers (the seigneurs de Lautrec and Lescun), Marshal La Palice, Montmorency, Chabot, Alençon, the Guise brothers and Florange, among many others.

In the short term, things went well for Francis, as they had done in 1515. He re-entered Lombardy and the duchy of Milan itself remarkably easily. The imperialists evacuated the city of Milan, allowing Francis to take possession of it peacefully. Instead, they occupied Pavia, the fortified city to the south on the banks of the Ticino, which Francis had himself easily occupied a decade earlier. Having done so then, Francis knew very well that he had to prevent his enemy counter-attacking from the city. As one report received in England put it, 'Bourbon, the viceroy of Naples, and the marquis of Pescara are at Cremona, Piacenza, and [Lodi] and may give the King some trouble if he do not take Pavia.'[9] The river flowed directly beneath the city walls on the south side, and the French first threw a semicircular siege line on the north bank from west to east. They eventually occupied an area called the

Borgo di Ticino to the south of the river as well, effectively encircling Pavia. They also occupied the extensive walled estate of the Castello Visconteo on the north side. The park contained a manor house, or *castello*, near its centre, called Mirabello.

The French began by using their artillery against Pavia's walls, followed by several unsuccessful sallies against the city. The imperial garrison of some 5,000–6,000 German and Spanish troops, under the command of Don Antonio de Leyva (1480–1536), held out against the initial French effort for far longer than Francis had anticipated. The king decided that, rather than retiring for the winter of 1524–5, he would remain in command of what was rapidly becoming a conventional siege. The strategic logic of his remaining was questionable, but, given his own success a decade earlier and the lack of it among his generals since then, Francis reasoned that this was an operation he had to direct personally. Active fighting in and around the siege drew to a halt as winter came on, and the imperialists were reinforced in January by 12,000 *Landsknechts* under the overall command of Georg von Frundsberg of Mindelheim (1473–1528).

Francis used the time over the winter to try to build diplomatic support, and Clement VII responded to the king's overtures by agreeing that he would not side with Charles. The pope requested that, in return, the king send some of his troops south to take hold of the kingdom of Naples. Rather than wanting the French actually to take the kingdom, Clement wished to assert papal authority over it against Charles. Despite the misgivings of some of his commanders, Francis assented and despatched John Stewart, Duke of Albany (c. 1482–1536), with some 600 men-at-arms and 4,000 infantry, south in furtherance of the pope's suggestion. Although he was reinforced by some 2,000 infantrymen and a similar number of *arquebusiers* under the command of the pope's nephew Giovanni de' Medici (1498–1526), the decision to send so many of his experienced infantrymen to Naples may have played a part in what followed. Estimates are necessarily imprecise, but the consensus from sources is that at this time, even with the withdrawal of troops to Naples, the two armies were roughly similar in size and disposition, but the imperial numbers were slightly fewer than the French. Francis's army comprised 1,000 lances of *gens d'armes* (that is, about 4,000 heavy cavalry and 2,000 pages and servants); 7,000 Swiss mercenaries (including 700 *arquebusiers*); 4,000 *Landsknechts* (including the 'Black Band' of Guelderland); 4,000 French and Gascon infantry (including 2,000 *arquebusiers*); 2,000 Italian *arquebusiers* and 2,000 other French and Italian light cavalry. Lannoy and Bourbon between them commanded a cavalry force of about 800 lances of mixed men-at-arms, drawn from across Charles v's European dominions, and 1,500 mixed Spanish and Italian light cavalry. The core of its infantry force were the 12,000 *Landsknechts* (who included 1,500 *arquebusiers*). They were supported by 5,000 Spanish infantry (of whom approximately 1,700 were *arquebusiers*) and 3,000 Italian *arquebusiers*. In addition, de Leyva's garrison in Pavia itself had about 30 lances of Spanish men-at-arms, 3,000 Spanish infantry (including approximately 1,000 *arquebusiers*), 5,000–6,000 *Landsknechts* (of whom 800 were *arquebusiers*) and about 1,000 Pavian city militia.[10]

In January 1525 the imperialist commanders made various attempts to raise the siege by luring the French into open battle. None worked directly, but towards the end of the month the imperialists occupied territory to the east of the main French camp, and Visconti Park on the eastern side of Pavia, effectively hemming the French in on that side and establishing a block on movement north or east of Pavia. In effect, the besiegers of Pavia were themselves besieged. With money running out and his troops ever restive, Lannoy decided to settle the issue. He launched a plan that he and his commanders had hatched to capture Francis, whom they believed (wrongly) to be headquartered at Mirabello in the centre of the park. The plan was also to make contact with the garrison in Pavia, in the hope that, with support from within the park, it could sally out and the combined imperial action would break the siege.

During the night of 23 February imperialist sappers broke down sections of the park walls at its northern end, and in the early hours of the morning of 24 February a force of cavalry and infantry commanded by Alfonso d'Avalos d'Aquino, 2nd Marquis del Vasto (1502–1546), attacked the house of Mirabello. Forewarned about the possibility, or even anticipating such an attack, Francis was actually with his cavalry further north and west within the park. As Mirabello was taken, blocks of infantry under Bourbon, Lannoy and Frundsberg moved sequentially into the park and began marching south. Florange, who was in charge of 3,000 Swiss in a holding position at the base of Visconti Park, now advanced northwards to confront the first block of *Landsknechts*, with which they immediately engaged in an intense pike battle at about 6.30 in the morning.

What happened next is still the subject of conjecture, but a crucial factor was Pescara's order to d'Avalos to position in copses towards the north of the park about 1,000 infantry armed with *arquebuses*, some of whom had just taken Mirabello and were returning from there. The blocks of *Landsknechts*, meanwhile, continued marching down from the top of the park and on towards the Swiss. For a time, some French guns in the south of the park bombarded the imperialists with little effective reply from the enemy, but did not significantly slow their progress. Aware that the imperial cavalry was being positioned to protect the right flank of the infantry as it advanced down the park, and recalling his successes at Marignano, Francis gathered his *gendarmerie* for a cavalry charge directly towards the enemy horse. With Francis at their head, the French mounted noblemen smashed through the ranks of the light cavalry commanded by the marquis of Sant'Angelo (who was killed), and charged on into the heavy cavalry under

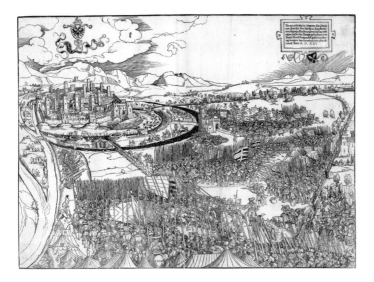

Lannoy. It, too, broke and retreated into the woodland at the top of the park. At this point Francis clearly thought he had won the day, shouting to Marshal de Foix as he charged, 'Monsieur Lescun, now I really am the Duke of Milan.' Presumably he now intended to regroup the cavalry and turn it directly against Frundsberg's German infantry, in support of the Swiss.

Francis and the *gendarmerie* were now about 550 metres (600 yd) from their starting point and the 4,000 *Landsknechts* of the Black Bands, and 2,000 Gascon infantry together under their commanders, François de Lorraine and Richard de la Pole. They were stationed to the south and west of the cavalry's starting point, awaiting orders to move in to support the king. As the French nobles came to the end of their charge, these infantry troops might have been signalled to move, but by that time the cavalry had also come within range of d'Avalos's *arquebusiers* concealed among the trees around and ahead of them in that section of the park, obscured perhaps by the poor light and mist of a winter's early morning. The Spanish riflemen opened fire. Although early

Jörg Breu the Elder, *The Battle of Pavia*, c. 1525, woodcut.

arquebus balls could not pierce armour at its thickest points, there were still plenty of targets they could hit on the bodies of the French knights and their horses. In their hundreds the cavalrymen were shot dead or wounded in their saddles, or thrown from them as their horses were killed or wounded, bringing them crashing to the ground.

As the *arquebusiers* kept up a raking fire on the French knights, the first block of imperial *Landsknechts* pushed the Swiss, who had marched up the park to confront them, back on themselves, and the Swiss looked likely to break. Frundsberg, in personal command of the second block, was therefore in a position to respond to Pescara's urgent request for support by turning his infantrymen west, partly to outflank the Swiss, but also in support of d'Avalos's *arquebusiers*. At about the same time Bourbon and his men-at-arms, and a third block of infantry that had initially moved west across the top of the park, turned and came south, down on to the left flank of the near-stationary French cavalry.

Alerted by the gunfire and the retreating elements at the rear of the French cavalry, Lorraine and Pole advanced with the Black Band and the Gascon infantry to try to help Francis and the *gendarmerie* in the forward positions, by engaging the flank of Frundsberg's *Landsknechts* as it turned westwards. They were, however, quickly caught 'as between tongs' by their German opponents. The Black Band was killed virtually to its last man, with Lorraine, Pole and nearly all the Gascons also dead. At about this time, and at a given signal, with the tide of the battle turning in its favour, the troops of the garrison at Pavia sortied and attacked the French encampments to the east of the city. They broke up the siege-works and in so doing also closed off the line of orderly retreat for the Swiss infantry then fighting in Visconti Park.[11]

Unlike at Marignano, where Francis had coordinated short cavalry charges very closely with the artillery and infantry movements, at Pavia he seems to have believed that one huge cavalry charge would carry all before it, if it raced to drive the imperial horse from the field. But this move had required his own artillery to cease fire, lessening the pressure on the *Landsknechts* bearing down on the Swiss. By contrast, Pescara's effective combination of *arquebusiers*, pikemen and cavalry was devastating and brought about a total collapse of French command. All order was lost. Later, Francis blamed his Swiss mercenaries for the defeat, but his own decision to charge when he did, in a win-or-lose gamble, was more significant. With the destruction of the French cavalry, the Swiss had no support against the relentless *Landsknechts*. They were also

Rupert Heller, *The Battle of Pavia*, c. 1529, oil on panel.

attacked from behind by the Pavia garrison and, not surprisingly, collapsed into disorderly retreat down the park. Emerging from it, they clashed with more elements of the Pavia garrison. Many plunged into the swollen and freezing waters of the Ticino, having found that the pontoon bridge the French had built had been destroyed by the troops sallying against their positions. Contemporary reports of the losses at Pavia, and historians' subsequent assessments of them, vary considerably. It is generally agreed that thousands of French men-at-arms were killed in battle or died shortly afterwards of their wounds or as they tried to escape across the Ticino, in what has aptly been described as the greatest slaughter of French noblemen in battle since Agincourt in 1415. Perhaps as many as 14,000 infantrymen died or were wounded, and thousands more were taken prisoner.

In the midst of the rout, Francis fought on until his horse was killed beneath him. He got to his feet, with his bodyguard mostly dead around him. He was surrounded by dismounted horsemen and foot soldiers, eagerly vying to capture him. He fought bravely and for some little time, but his cause was already lost. Casting wildly around him, Francis looked for someone of sufficient rank to whom he could surrender. Several men, including one La Mothe de Noyers, a captain in Bourbon's cavalry, later claimed that they had captured him. Eventually, Lannoy rode back, seeking as much to protect the king as to capture him, and Francis surrendered formally to the imperial viceroy, reputedly with the words, 'Don Charles, here is the sword of a king who has earned praise, because before giving it up he has spilled the blood of many of your men; so he has been taken prisoner, not through cowardice, but through ill fortune.'[12] He was escorted from the field and kept initially in Lannoy's command post before being taken to the Certosa of Pavia, northwards on the road to Milan. A few days later he was moved from there east to the fortified town of Pizzighettone on the Adda river, there to come to terms with the scale of his

defeat, and to write to his mother the words quoted at the outset
of this chapter.

The Battle of Pavia was fought on the morning of Charles V's
twenty-fifth birthday but it was not until 10 March, in the Alcázar
fortress at Madrid, that the emperor received news of the victory.
He did so with remarkable calm and withdrew to pray privately
for some time before emerging to receive the congratulations of
his courtiers. Francis spent the spring in Pizzighettone as Louise
and her regency council scrambled to provide defences for the
borders of the realm and to exercise any remaining diplomatic
strength France had in Italy and England, offering what could
be where it could be, and urging joint action against a now all-
powerful emperor. In May Lannoy escorted Francis to Genoa to
board a ship bound for Naples, where it was thought he could
be more securely held. Before it got underway, however, the plans
changed. Apparently at Francis's insistent suggestion, Lannoy
agreed to sail for Spain instead, passing close by the French coast
en route. Perhaps Francis wanted to escape the clutches of Bourbon
in Italy, feared imprisonment in Naples far from his kingdom,
or thought it might be best to meet Charles personally and resolve
their differences together; or all three. Prisoner he may have been,
but he was still accorded the respect due to one of the most powerful European monarchs, so Lannoy complied and Charles agreed.
Galleys were sent from France and Spanish crews put on board,
and the king was sailed to Spain.

Francis arrived in Barcelona in mid-June 1525 as something
of a star. Contemporaries attest that, at this point, the king seems
to have borne his captivity well and was gracious to all who
came to see and meet him as he made his way to Madrid in what
seemed more like a state visit than the transporting of a defeated
opponent. Perhaps Francis expected that his natural easy charm
would work its magic on the emperor as it had appeared to do
with Henry VIII at the Field of Cloth of Gold. If that was his

hope, it was very soon disappointed. Francis's principal advisor and companion in arms, Bonnivet, had been killed at Pavia, so the king turned to another childhood companion who would become the longest-serving and most important advisor of his reign, Anne de Montmorency. Already a marshal of France, Montmorency worked closely with the king's sister Marguerite in negotiations on his behalf and in consultation with Louise. This freed the regent to concentrate on domestic governance, to raise the enormous ransom that would be needed to bring her son home, and to conclude the war with England and arrange for one against the emperor in Italy.

Henry VIII had received the news of Pavia on or about 9 March with unabashed delight. He was especially pleased to learn that Pole, who called himself Earl of Suffolk, 'the white rose' and the last Yorkist claimant to the English crown, had been killed. Henry wanted immediately to divide France between himself and Charles in accordance with their agreement of 1522.[13] Yet Charles did not now wish to place so great a God-given victory at Pavia at the service of Henry's local ambitions. Instead, it was to be used, he said, to bring about a wider, permanent peace in Europe, but on his terms. In any case, during May 1525 the English people refused to pay the extra-parliamentary taxation, the so-called Amicable Grant, required to raise an army for any invasion of France. This combination of circumstances required Wolsey and Henry once more to contemplate the possibility of peace with France, something to which Wolsey was readily inclined. He renewed the negotiations with Louise's representatives and these culminated in the Treaty of the More, signed on 30 August 1525, which brought peace between England and France.[14]

With England no longer an enemy, and once again even a potential ally, Montmorency and Marguerite worked closely to arrive at as advantageous a settlement as possible with Charles. Negotiations with the emperor's council carried on through the autumn of 1525 at Toledo even as Francis suffered some sort of illness, the exact nature of which has not been identified fully. It seems to have been some kind of nasal abscess, together perhaps with exhaustion and anorexia, or possibly malarial fever (from which he nearly died, and recurring bouts of which he seems to have suffered for the rest of his life).[15] Charles's public talk of wanting to create European peace from his victory at Pavia was not wholly disingenuous, but he did want to make Francis pay for his folly and obstructive ambition, and to impose a *dis*advantageous settlement on him. He demanded nothing less than the duchy of Burgundy, which he claimed as heir to the patrimony of the Valois dukes of Burgundy, but which the French king regarded as a core part of his kingdom, an appanage repatriated by Louis XI after the death of the last Valois duke, Charles the Bold, in 1477. Louis had also taken the neighbouring, but separate, Franche-Comté or 'Free County' of Burgundy, but this had been given back to Philip of Burgundy, the grandson of Charles the Bold, by Charles VIII of France. Philip's father, Maximilian von Habsburg, had accepted the county at Philip's death in 1506, and had in turn passed it to his grandson Charles V. The status of Franche-Comté was never contested by Francis (and it was to there that Bourbon had fled in 1523), but he was determined to resist the claim to the duchy of Burgundy proper.

Charles also insisted that Francis give up all his claims on the Italian peninsula. This was no more acceptable to Francis than returning Burgundy. Yet Charles never resiled from his opening position. In order, therefore, to gain his freedom as soon as he wanted, Francis had to capitulate to the emperor's demands – or at least appear to do so. The Treaty of Madrid was signed on 14 January 1526. Burgundy was conceded whole to Charles, and Francis gave up all his claims in Italy and on the counties of Flanders and Artois. Francis also agreed to give his two eldest sons, François and Henri, as hostages for his performance of the treaty obligations. Finally, the treaty was to be confirmed by his marriage to Charles's sister Eleanor, who had formerly been promised to Bourbon. The duke himself was to be reinstated and his lands secured.[16]

News of the likely 'settlement' Charles wished to impose on Francis had been shared with potential allies in Italy and with Wolsey, who was aghast. He wrote that the king should not regard himself as bound by such a dishonourable agreement, and had already begun talks for a new alliance. Pope Clement saw the agreement as unworkable and expressed himself at least well disposed towards France. Louise lost no time in playing on such support to build a coalition in Italy, headed by Venice. Lannoy, Louise and Montmorency all did their level best to assure the emperor that Francis would keep his word about the treaty. Knowing by then that he was not as isolated as he appeared, Francis had already come to a decision himself. Two days before signing the treaty, he made a private declaration under oath that he would never surrender Burgundy.[17]

The treaty having been signed, Charles met Francis for a few days in Madrid in February 1526, and Francis met his prospective wife for the first time. It was another month, however, before all the arrangements were in place for his release, including the exchange of the king for his two sons. This took place on 17 March 1526 near Fuenterrabía, on a pontoon in the middle of the Bidassoa river, which marked the border between France and Spain. Francis could have only a very brief meeting with his sons as they crossed, but he promised that he would fetch them home again as soon as possible. He rode from the border to Bayonne, where he was met by his mother. The city's bells rang out and guns fired in salute from its walls.

THE RETURN OF THE KING

In May 1526 an alliance was formed by the League of Cognac, concluded between France, Pope Clement VII, Florence, Sforza Milan and Venice. Although Wolsey had urged its formation, at the last minute England did not join but agreed only to be the league's 'sponsor'. This strained but did not break relations with Charles – just as Wolsey intended. Once more he sought to position Henry as the indifferent 'arbiter' between the opponents, while limiting his financial contribution to the enterprise. Fighting broke out in Italy once more, and Wolsey began direct negotiations with Francis for a renewed and separate Anglo-French alliance.

The kingdom did its best to show the expected jubilation at the ruler's return, once Lent had finished and as Francis travelled via his home town of Cognac to the Loire Valley. The surprising truth was that, for all the trauma suffered by the king himself after Pavia, France had managed well enough without him for almost eighteen months. Arrangements had been put in place and the nobility, the cities and the institutions of the state, such as the provincial *parlements*, had rubbed along together, albeit with friction at times. They had complained of the regency, and to the regent. Yet in the king's absence they had also got things done, and in most of France life had gone on pretty much as normal. Paris had perhaps felt his absence most. It had suffered the threat of English attack at times, and the absence of the court had disrupted businesses as varied as printing, transportation and fashion. The general climate of uncertainty and the need to raise money for the king's ransom did not make for good business, and disrupted trade routes during a state of war between France, the Netherlands and the German lands had not helped either.

It was therefore incumbent upon Francis at his return to reanimate his kingship, restore confidence in his command of the kingdom and ensure the smooth running of its daily commerce,

Jean Clouet, *Francis I*, 1526, oil on panel.

agrarian and artisanal industries. For that, he had also to resurrect
the authority and solemnity, as well as the glamour and celebrity,
of his court. He had to reassert his personal authority and make
himself once more the fount of favour and patronage for the members of the political nation. This was no simple task. He was no
longer quite the fresh-faced *jeune premier* and darling of the nobility
that he had been at his accession a decade earlier. A great many
noblemen had been killed in battle in a foolish war that Francis
had begun, the consequences of which still threatened the integrity
of the kingdom. He would have to find a degree of maturity, focus
and purpose in governing France that he had not previously demonstrated. Perhaps it was these qualities that the portrait of the
king made by Jean Clouet in 1526 was intended to show.

Francis's altered personal circumstances at his return reinforced the sense of necessary change. Queen Claude had died in
July 1524, just a few months short of her twenty-fifth birthday,
and very soon after her husband had left the Loire to confront
Bourbon and pursue his second campaign for Milan. The cause
of her death is not known, but she had given her husband seven
children in eight years. It has been suggested that she never prop-
erly recovered from the birth of Marguerite in June 1523. In
November 1526 her body – with that of Princess Charlotte, who
had died at the age of six only a few months after her mother –
was brought, with great solemnity, for reburial at the basilica of
Saint-Denis. In keeping with royal custom, Francis did not attend
the obsequies, but arrived back in Paris shortly afterwards, for
the first time in almost three years. The king did at least have the
consolation of his two youngest daughters and his youngest son.
Set against that was the anxiety induced by his eldest sons being
held in Spain, in conditions that were at times barely tolerable for
boys of their status.[18]

To grapple with this situation, a new generation of advisors
now came to the fore alongside such stalwarts as Duprat, replacing

some who had died in the war. The new Admiral of France in succession to Guillaume Bonnivet was Philippe Chabot, seigneur de
Brion (*c.* 1492–1543). He also received a gift of 40,000 *livres* from
the king, and the governorship of Burgundy. Undoubtedly the
most important new advisor, however, was Anne de Montmorency,
upon whom the office of *Grand Maître* (Great Master) of France,
responsible for the overall working of the royal household, was
conferred in March 1526. In 1527 he married Madeleine, daughter
of the king's uncle René de Savoie, former *Grand Maître*, who had
been killed at Pavia. Montmorency was thereby brought into the
extended royal family, becoming a cousin of the king and a nephew
of Louise.

During those years, Montmorency increasingly advocated
the resolution of the conflict and the pursuit of peaceful relations
with Charles v as consistent with Francis's interests. Yet, like
Chabot, in the spring of 1526 he opposed the implementation
of the Madrid treaty. It was out of the question that Burgundy
should be handed over to the emperor. Encouraged by the prospect of an anti-imperial alliance, Francis and his new advisors
delayed ratifying the treaty and sought to formulate a legal basis
for his refusal to be bound by it. It was not within his power, Francis
told Charles, to give away part of France, because to do so would
contravene his coronation oath and the fundamental laws of
France that protected its integrity. In this determination, he ensured that he had the support of the provincial estates of Burgundy,
ably assisted by Chabot, the recently appointed royal governor,
who also inspected fortifications to ensure Charles could not
take the duchy by force.

Perhaps the French ought not to have worried too much. At
about this time Charles wrote to his brother Ferdinand in Austria
that he was keen finally to secure not Burgundy proper, but
Lombardy and Milan, but alas had insufficient funds to do so.[19]
Before long, however, there was an even bigger threat to Habsburg

interests. In the summer of 1526 the Ottoman Sultan Süleyman 'the Magnificent' (or the Lawgiver; 1494/5–1566) invaded Hungary. In August he won a crushing victory at Mohács, in the retreat from which King Louis II of Hungary (1506–1526) was killed as he fell from his horse. Through his marriage to their sister Mary of Habsburg (1505–1558), Louis had been brother-in-law to Charles and Ferdinand (1503–1564). The latter had pleaded for Charles's help to safeguard Hungary, but the emperor had said that he was in no position to do anything militarily against the Ottoman sultan. He felt he must secure Italy before he could do anything more. After the serious outcome of Mohács, there was little strategically to be done against the Ottomans anyway.[20]

The year 1527 began at the French court with the marriage in January of Marguerite to her second husband, Henri II, king of Navarre, at Saint-Germain-en-Laye. Twelve years younger than Marguerite, and her personal choice as husband, Henri was acceptable to Francis as a brother-in-law because he was a king, albeit a disadvantaged one. He was somewhat more culturally sophisticated than her first husband, and a hero (if that is the right word) as a survivor of Pavia, and their marriage was initially happy. In 1528 Marguerite gave birth to a daughter, Jeanne (1528–1572), who would in a short time, like her mother before her, be involved in Francis's political ambitions. But Marguerite soon became bored with the provincial court of Navarre and with her young husband's philandering. While hardly a model husband himself, Francis demanded that Henri treat his sister more respectfully.

Charles V's relations with Bourbon had by then become strained. Although nominated by Charles as duke of Milan, and still an imperial commander in charge of a sizeable body of mercenary troops, Bourbon was in fact a penniless exile, whose native lands had been seized by the French crown, something about which Charles could apparently do nothing. His debts to his troops

François Clouet (attrib.), *Marguerite de Navarre*, c. 1540, oil on panel.

the diminished resources of Milan could not supply. Growing increasingly desperate, Bourbon turned towards the only power in Italy that could provide money in the short term: the pope in Rome. Accordingly, he began marching his troops south, intent on some intimidatory bargaining with Clement (who had by then virtually abandoned the League of Cognac anyway) about paying his army's arrears. As he marched south, the Florentines rose up again and threw the Medici out, re-establishing the Republic for a final time. Within weeks a huge force of unpaid, rebellious German troops, many of them perhaps inspired by what they had (mis)understood of Luther's criticism of the papacy, drew near to Christendom's capital.

Meanwhile Wolsey, with the enthusiastic support of Louise and Montmorency, was moving England rapidly into a full alliance with France. Negotiations reached their peak in February and were concluded in the Treaty of Westminster, which was signed on 30 April 1527. In return for what would soon be called the 'Eternal Peace' between England and France, Francis affirmed a total debt to Henry of 2 million crowns and a share in the revenues of the *gabelle* or salt tax. In effect, Francis bought Henry out of his claim to France. Princess Mary, formerly betrothed to the dauphin, would now be the bride either of Francis himself or of Henri d'Orléans. Celebratory festivities that deliberately recalled the extravagance of the Field of Cloth of Gold were held for the French signatories to the treaty at Greenwich and in London in May 1527. They were at their height when news reached England that Rome had been sacked by imperial troops and the pope himself forced to take refuge in the Castel Sant'Angelo.[21]

Bourbon was killed scaling the walls of Rome, and his death unleashed an unbridled attack on the population of the city and the plunder of its wealth, in which as many as 8,000 citizens may have died. Francis received the news shortly after his rather low-key return to Paris. In July, Cardinal Wolsey was welcomed to

France as the 'Cardinal Peacemaker'. In meetings with Francis at Amiens and Compiègne, the peace agreement made in April was expanded into a fuller and apparently permanent Anglo-French alliance. Henri d'Orléans was confirmed as the future husband of Princess Mary, and Francis's marriage to Eleanor of Portugal was accepted by Henry. By August a new French army was on its way to Milan under Marshal Lautrec. It invaded Lombardy, but Francis ordered his general to bypass Milan itself and press on to Naples. With Clement still in captivity, the French march south could be presented as a rescue effort, or at least an attempt to secure the pope's safety, from the malign forces of the emperor. Alfonso I d'Este, Duke of Ferrara (1476–1534), also joined the anti-imperial campaign. His son Ercole (1508–1559) was promised to Renée de France in marriage.

While in France, Wolsey had also told Francis for the first time of Henry's wish to have his marriage to Katherine of Aragon annulled. He did so, hoping to secure the cooperation of the French king and the cardinals of the Curia for a plan whereby he, Wolsey, would superintend the Church during the pope's captivity. During his 'vicarate' he would of course approve the annulment. Whatever Francis thought of such a plan, Henry himself grew impatient of this elaborate and difficult conjunction. Henry sent his own representative, William Knight, to Rome, effectively behind Wolsey's back. There he demanded the annulment, but he – and other English representatives who followed – did so in such a way as to alert the Curia to Henry's real intentions in respect of Anne Boleyn. This was something Wolsey had tried desperately to avoid. The French regime quickly saw the potential of Henry's marriage problem for creating disharmony between him and Charles, and promised Henry every support. Francis joined Henry in demanding the pope's release and that of the two French princes in Spain. Charles refused, and in January 1528 the two kings, now members of each other's orders of chivalry and calling each other

'good brother, friend and perpetual ally', jointly declared war on
Charles.[22]

Perhaps unsurprisingly the French campaign in Italy in 1528–9
was no more successful than any since 1521. Lautrec was initially
assisted by the Genoese mercenary naval captain Andrea Doria
(1466–1560), who commanded his nephew Filippino to assist

Francis I's ratification of the Treaty of Westminster at Amiens, 18 August 1527.

the French as they laid siege to Naples by land and sea. Things went well initially, but Andrea was angered that Francis was slow to pay him and by the king's refusal of a number of territorial claims Andrea made. At length, the mercenary captain decided to accept Charles's secret overtures to become his admiral of the Mediterranean, and ordered his nephew to lift the naval blockade. Soon afterwards, plague broke out in the French camp at Naples, taking hundreds with it, including Lautrec. By September Genoa had also revolted against Francis, throwing out the French garrison there. The following year François de Bourbon, comte de Saint-Pol, was sent to recover Genoa, but he was defeated at the Battle of Landriano in June 1529. At this point Clement VII, showing unusual decisiveness, broke finally with the League of Cognac and was reconciled with Charles under the Treaty of Barcelona. The Medici were thereby restored to power in Florence and Clement invited Charles to enter Italy to be crowned emperor. Once more, Francis's efforts by military means to establish power in Italy and to compel Charles to accept his dynastic claims there had failed. He was forced by events, and encouraged by Montmorency, to try a new approach and seek instead a comprehensive diplomatic resolution with Charles.

The emperor's attitude had also changed since the days of quiet exultation and high expectation in the aftermath of Pavia. Francis could not simply be swept aside from, nor swept along with, the great project of Charles's imagined imperial destiny. Rather, he would have to be tolerated first, and bargained with next, to dissuade him from opposing Charles's chivalric aims, at least against the Protestant princes and Süleyman, and to come to a reasonable settlement of their disputes. And that is what Charles seems to have been prepared to do in the summer of 1529, especially now that he and Clement were reconciled and allied. His hope was that he would thereby secure his control on Milan and of Lombardy generally. The strategic importance of this area

for shipping troops, money and supplies from Spain or Naples
to northern Italy, Austria, Germany, Hungary and the Netherlands
as necessary was daily becoming more obvious.

Thus was convened a remarkable set of peace talks presided
over by two remarkable women: Francis's mother, by then 53, and
Charles's paternal aunt Margaret of Austria, aged 49. Both women
shared a lifelong commitment to peace. They were sisters-in-law
and had met as girls at the French court during the minority of
Charles VIII. At one point Margaret, the step-granddaughter
of Margaret of York, was to have married Charles, but he chose to
marry Anne de Bretagne instead. Some time later, Margaret married Louise's brother Philibert II, duc de Savoie (1480–1504).
When he died, aged only 24, Margaret returned to the Netherlands,
where she represented her father, Maximilian, and helped to raise
her nephew Charles of Burgundy and his siblings at her palace
at Mechelen. At Charles's accession to the Iberian crowns, Margaret
became his regent in the Netherlands, and both his chancellors,
Mercurino di Gattinara and then Antoine Perrenot de Granvelle
(1517–1586), entered Charles's service on her recommendation.

Although strictly an imperial city, Cambrai was well defended
and regarded as neutral for meeting purposes. The two large
entourages arrived on 4 July. Duprat and Montmorency escorted
Louise and the queen of Navarre, who had tried to mediate in the
negotiations in Spain. Both parties wanted to reach a settlement
quickly and free from outside interference, especially that of the
English, who, in the person of Wolsey, sought to involve themselves
as mediators. Charles and Francis therefore deliberately misled
Henry, through their ambassadors, as to the seriousness of the
talks and their chances of success. Wolsey was, in any case, stuck
during the summer of 1529 in the ultimately futile proceedings of
the legatine court at Blackfriars, hearing Henry's annulment case.
Henry was represented instead at the talks by Cuthbert Tunstall
and Sir Thomas More.

Negotiations continued for nearly a month involving representatives from Venice, Milan, Florence, the papacy and England, and a treaty was finally agreed and sworn to by Louise and Margaret on 5 August 1529. Its main terms were that Charles would concede the duchy of Burgundy to Francis in return for an indemnity of 2 million crowns, to be paid partly through settling 290,000 crowns of imperial debt to the English. Francis was to remove his troops from Italy and surrender all his claims there in line with the treaty of 1526. He was also to proceed with his marriage to Eleanor. French suzerainty over the counties of Flanders and Artois was to be conceded to the emperor. In return, Charles was to release the two princes of France and to surrender rights over various counties and lordships along the Somme. Francis was also to supply money and galleys to assist Charles's journey to Italy for his coronation – a journey he had begun even before the treaties were signed, a fact that may indicate his belief in their ultimate success. Francis ratified the treaty in Paris on 20 October, witnessed by, among others, Anne's brother Sir George Boleyn (c. 1504–1536). As both imperial and French ambassadors in England told their masters, Anne was now daily in the company of Henry VIII. At the last, Wolsey made difficulties about ratifying the English participation in the treaty, still hoping to wrest something more out of it for Henry and himself – for, with the failure of the legatine court to resolve the annulment issue, his need was great. At the end of the same month, he was dismissed as chancellor. The English king ratified the treaty at Greenwich in November.

The so-called Ladies' Peace of 1529 had its critics, not least in Venice and Milan, because it seemed to hand the whole Italian peninsula over to Charles and the papacy. It did not bring about genuine trust or affection between Charles and Francis. Nevertheless, it worked better than the Madrid treaty it was intended to rectify. It was no more 'perpetual' than any other agreement of the time, but it lasted for six years, the longest period of

Franco-Imperial accord during Francis's reign. In the spring of 1530 Francis and Louise travelled to Bayonne to oversee the return of the dauphin François and his brother Henri to France. The pair were eventually released by Charles in July, after payment of the ransom money. The princes once more crossed the Bidassoa and went thence to Saint-Jean-de-Luz. Queen Eleanor also crossed into France, escorted by the Cardinal François de Tournon, who was just then rising in status and authority in Francis's regime (see Chapter Four). She and Francis met at Roquefort-de-Marsan on 3 July. Although already married by proxy, they underwent a second, personal, ceremony at the nearby monastery of Saint-Laurent de Beyries four days later. From there, the royal couple travelled to Bordeaux, where the new queen of France made the first of many formal entries to the principal towns of the realm. Louise met her new daughter-in-law and travelled with her and her grandchildren and the king up to Cognac and then on to Amboise by late September.[23]

Very little time remained to Louise. At the end of 1530 came news that Margaret of Austria, with whom she had worked so closely on the great peace of the previous year, had died. Louise had expended all her energies in serving her son's kingship. She had long suffered from painful gout and was reported to be ill with it, and with colic and stomach pains, in December 1530. She had, nevertheless, recovered sufficiently to accompany her son at the coronation of Queen Eleanor at Saint-Denis the following spring. Louise spent the summer of 1531 at Fontainebleau with her son and daughter. Francis moved on, but the two women remained. Marguerite sent frequent letters to her brother, making him aware that as the seasons changed, his mother's health was again in decline. Plague soon broke out in the area, and Marguerite accompanied Louise south towards the Loire. But she could go no further than Grez-sur-Loing, from where Marguerite advised Montmorency, who was then hosting the king at Chantilly, that the end was near. Louise did not see Francis, her 'Caesar', again. She died on 22 September, aged 55. 'Our trinity', as Marguerite once called it, was dissolved. Louise's death deprived Francis of her support, but she bequeathed to him the lands and titles she had by marriage and those that he had given her as king. This included a large portion of the Bourbon patrimony, comprising Auvergne, Forez, Marche, Montpensier and Clermont. Her obsequies began at the abbey of Saint-Maur-des-Fossés and concluded in great solemnity, with royal ceremony and honours, at Notre-Dame in Paris and at Saint-Denis, where she was interred on 19 October 1531.

Opinion on Louise remains divided. Nineteenth- and some twentieth-century historians (all male, of course) tended to be critical. She was seen as keeping Francis too long tied to her apron strings, even of making him dependent on her. She was also accused of personal avarice. Her conduct towards the rights and lands of Charles de Bourbon in 1523–6 certainly demonstrated mixed motives. The same is true of her less-than-charitable involvement in the destruction of Semblançay (see Chapter Three). On the other hand, historians have more recently celebrated her record as a woman exercising public power in a patriarchal society. She is credited, surely rightly, with adroitness in using that power in her son's interests and, generally, those of his realm. She seems to have offered sound advice, often restraining his more bellicose ambitions in the furtherance of peace, while also understanding that workable peace was secured only with advantage (however conceived) to his chivalric reputation. As Francis's regent in 1525–6, Louise had all but saved his monarchy when she negotiated peace with England, helped to organize anti-imperial action in Italy, and constrained a somewhat reluctant kingdom to raise the ransom demanded by the Treaty of Madrid in order to free her son. Three years later, with her cousin Margaret of Austria, she had re-engineered that agreement into something that gave

Francis greater freedom of movement against Charles, and the period of his closest cooperation and friendship with Henry of England.

The education Louise had overseen for Francis and the love of the arts that she instilled in him added to her own reputation as well as his, and it is hard to imagine her not having enjoyed direct influence on his patronage as king. She was no saint, but, as ambassadors from throughout Europe noted, Louise was an astute politician and worked as hard as she could in every sphere for her son's interests. Only with her death, it might be argued, did her 'Caesar' truly begin his personal rule as king of France. Francis expressed his profound sense of loss and obligation to her in a moving epitaph, one of whose telling stanzas reads:

> You, who have beaten disaster triumphant,
> Saving our honour, our peace, and your own son,
> In war upholding, with peace re-found,
> By your great virtue and guidance sound.[24]

THREE

Francis as Governor and Patron

But what is more, [the king] knew most of the gentlemen
of good houses of his kingdom and spoke very well of
their origins and genealogies; and of those whom he saw
had become poor, had pity on them and assisted them,
saying that nothing in the world was so miserable as rich
becoming poor. It was also astonishing how he could
at once sustain the great expenses of war, as well as his
generosity (especially and greatly towards women), the
ceremonies, luxuries and munificence of his court, and
his superb buildings.[1]

So Pierre de Bourdeille, the seigneur de Brantôme,
characterized Francis's attitude towards his nobles. He
emphasized the king's detailed knowledge of their
ancestries, their family's present circumstances and individual
interests. He gilded the lily somewhat in order to contrast Francis's
record as a 'proper' patron of the nobility with that of his three
grandsons and successors, whom Brantôme blamed for losing
the esteem in which the crown was once held. During the second
decade of his reign, with the disaster of Pavia and his captivity
behind him, recovering and maintaining the support of the
nobility, and with it his royal authority, was vital for Francis. It
was in that decade that he began to exercise his personal rule as

Joos van Cleve, *Francis I*, c. 1532–3, oil on panel.

king more amply and directly than ever, especially after the death in 1531 of his foremost advisor and supporter, his mother, Louise.

THE 'PERSONAL RULE' OF FRANCIS

During the first decade of Francis's reign, the royal court had been the principal means by which the new king had established his personal authority and his reputation as a 'Renaissance' monarch. He had used offices in the royal household to attract nobles of all ages and ranks to his service, and through them to build a personal network of supporters, sometimes called a 'clientage' or an 'affinity', based on the one he had first created through his status as comte d'Angoulême and heir presumptive to Louis XII. That had not, perhaps, been as wide or as important among high French noble society as those of the great dukes of the Bourbon dynasty or other aristocrats, but once he was king, Francis's affinity had grown quickly and, over time, eclipsed all others. As this happened, he created new accommodation for the court, such as that at Blois, and cultivated a mix of impressive formality in court ceremonial at times, as well as a winning spontaneity in his personal encounters with nobles. It was much the same story at his return to France from Spain in the spring of 1526, but on a much larger scale and with further-reaching consequences. As regent, Louise had maintained her own household and council at Lyon so as to be near her son when he was in Milan, and during his absence in Spain, the French court had effectively gone into abeyance. With Francis's return, it revived rapidly and grew steadily in size, organization and personnel. Estimates of overall numbers are notoriously difficult, and we should distinguish the court in its widest sense, which may have contained as many as 10,000 people at particular times (such as the Field of Cloth of Gold in 1520), from the regular salaried royal household, which contained about 540 people in 1523 and half as many again by the mid-1540s.

The three main departments of the royal household were the *Chapelle*, the *Chambre* and the *Hôtel*. The *Chapelle* was under the formal authority of the *Grand Aumônier de France*, a title created by Francis. Under the Aumônier, the *Chapelle* tended to the king's spiritual needs and those of the court with confessors, chaplains, musicians and several choirs, who sang Mass and kept other religious observations. Francis's former tutor, François Demoulins, became Aumônier in 1519. He was succeeded in that post in 1526 (by when he is presumed to have died) by Jean Le Veneur, bishop of Lisieux (*c.* 1473–1543). The *Chambre* was the department responsible for the king's personal accommodation in the several rooms of his private apartments, including the *chambre* itself. It consisted of several sub-departments responsible for the king's clothes and effects, whose personnel, the *gentilshommes de la chambre*, took care of his day-to-day needs, helping him to dress and keeping him company during leisure time and so on. The *chambre* also included those who served the king his meals, as well as his physicians, apothecaries, secretaries and the *valets de chambre*. These last could be lower-ranked nobles in service, but under Francis the post of *valet* was increasingly filled by his artisan tailors, furriers, shoemakers, painters, instrument-makers and so on. Eventually a separate office was created for them, the king's *gens de métier*.

The *Hôtel* was the 'below stairs', or outermost, part of the court, encompassing all the other services the royal family and entourage needed, but principally its feeding. It comprised the *paneterie*, *échansonnerie* and *fruiterie*, and had two kitchens, the *cuisine de bouche* for the king and the *cuisine de commun*, which fed the court officers. The departments of the *écurie*, *vénerie* and *fauconnerie* were collectively responsible for the king's horses, transport and security, his hunting dogs and birds respectively. The larger court's movements and lodging were the responsibility of the *fourrière*, whose officers, the *maréschaux de logis*, found accommodation and shelter and oversaw supplies when the court was on the move. These departments were variously staffed by a mix of noble and common servants, each under one of the supervising *maîtres d'hôtel*.

The entire royal household was overseen by the *Grand Maître de France*, who from 1526 was, as we have seen, Francis's close friend and advisor Anne de Montmorency. Montmorency was already the king's leading body servant as the *premier gentilhomme de la chambre*, and his appointment made him a major political figure in France. He now outranked in authority and influence with the king even the great aristocrats of the realm whose titles were higher than his as a baron. He used this power to bring into the royal circle men of promise at all social levels, from fellow nobles to secretaries, chaplains and artisans. His influence in these years was built almost entirely on his personal friendship with the king and the apparent success of his foreign policy. In addition to the family's lands in the Île-de-France, centred on its seats at Chantilly and Écouen, and at La Rochepot in Burgundy, he obtained estates in Brittany and played an active part in establishing direct royal authority in central-southern France. Montmorency was also made governor of Languedoc in 1526. From this position he recruited noblemen as commanders in the heavy cavalry, as knights of the royal order of chivalry, as town governors and as captains of castles and strategically important ports.[2]

One very important mechanism in attracting clients to direct royal service seems to have been the enhancement and clarification of the status of offices that gave regular access to the king, and particularly that of *gentilhomme de la chambre*, an office developed by Francis himself at his accession. From 1527 its potential to enhance the crown's ability to manipulate personal and patrimonial connections across the realm seems to have been more fully realized. The *gentilshommes* were raised in the order of precedence for all public occasions, appearing after ambassadors and the judges of the *parlements*. Their wages were increased far above those of any other court office – although admittedly still modest at

1,200 *livres* a year – and their names now headed the annual royal
household payment rolls, after those of the clergy.[3] These changes
reinforced Montmorency's preponderant (although never ex-
clusive) influence upon Francis. Among the appointees to these
posts were the men who were part of the first generation of those
known to the king and in his chamber service, or their relatives.
Montmorency aside, this group included Admiral Philippe Chabot
and Jean de Genouillac *dit* Galiot, captain-general of the artillery,
who was made *Grand Écuyer de France* in succession to Galeazzo da
San Severino, who had been killed at Pavia. Chamber and table
servants in this group included Antoine de Raffin, seigneur de
Pecavalry, noted in England as early as 1518 as a great favourite of
the king, and Jean de Dinteville (1504–1555), an ambassador to
England and depicted as such by Hans Holbein in his famous
painting *The Ambassadors* (1533). In this group were also the brothers
Antoine, François and Louis de Rochechouart-Mortemart, for-
bears of the marquise de Montespan, a mistress of Louis XIV. The
group also included the sons or brothers of others killed at Pavia,
such as Claude and Honorat de Savoie, sons of the king's uncle
René. Claude de Savoie, comte de Tende (1507–1566) succeeded
his father as governor of Provence in 1525 and held the post for
the remainder of Francis's reign.[4]

The preponderant influence of Montmorency himself is
undeniable. Research has established the extraordinary landed
fortune he amassed in working closely with the king to shorten
and straighten lines of communication and patronage. He created a network that reinforced existing ties between himself and
the *clienteles* of the oldest families and great nobles, as well as with
newer men.[5] As well as his connection by marriage to Louise de
Savoie's family, Montmorency was linked with the counts of
Laval through the marriage of his sister (also, confusingly, called
Anne) to Guy XVI de Laval (1476–1531), who had assisted Louise
de Savoie during her regency. On Francis's return from Spain,

Laval was named governor of Brittany, finally eclipsing his main
Breton rivals the Rohans. At Guy's death in 1531, Montmorency
brought his nephew Guy XVII to court, who, within three years –
while still in his mid-teens – had been made a *gentilhomme de la
chambre*.[6] Montmorency also arranged the young Guy's marriage
to Claude de Foix (1526–1553), heiress to the house of Foix-
Lautrec, thereby strengthening Montmorency's own ties with
the extended Foix family. It was then among the most illustrious
in royal service, and already well represented in the household.
Guy spent the remainder of the 1530s in the royal household and
in the entourage of the future Henri II, where he was joined by
his kinsman Louis V de Rohan, seigneur de Guéméné (1513–1557).
The crown's favour to the Lavals, and indeed to the Rohans and
other local clans, was not unrelated to its successful effort to have
the Breton estates, the *Grands Jours*, accept the incorporation of
the duchy into the crown of France through recognizing the
dauphin François, grandson of Anne de Bretagne, as duke. That
process was formally completed in August 1532.[7]

Montmorency was also closely involved in bringing the lands
of the disgraced duc de Bourbon directly into the Valois royal
affinity. Several of the *gentilshommes de la chambre* were involved in,
and profited by, seizing lands, assets and offices once controlled
by the duke. Most prominent among them was Jean d'Albon,
seigneur de Saint-André (1472–1549), who had been a prominent client of Charles de Bourbon but had also served in Francis's
Italian campaigns. By 1530 he was appointed a knight of the
Order of Saint-Michel and a *gentilhomme de la chambre*. He thereafter assisted Montmorency in raising money in the Bourbonnais
to secure the release of Francis's sons, and was appointed governor of the person of the future Henri II. D'Albon's more famous son Jacques (*c.* 1505–1562), the future marshal, was placed
in Henri's household and first appeared on the muster rolls of
his father's cavalry company in 1531. In 1539 Jean was made royal

governor of the formerly semi-independent Bourbon heartland
of the Lyonnais.

David Potter has shown that in the frontier province of Picardy,
the *gentilshommes de la chambre* were also involved in keeping an eye
on (to put it no stronger than that) the deceased Constable's
cousin Charles, duc de Vendôme (1489–1537), who was the paramount aristocrat there. Here, too, Montmorency connections
were important. Charles retained the governorship of the province, which he had held since 1519, and was far from a marginal-
ized figure, but he was not entirely trusted by those closest to
the king, including Marguerite de Navarre. In May 1531 it was
not a Bourbon adherent but Montmorency's younger brother,
François, seigneur de La Rochepot (1496/8–1551), who succeeded
Vendôme's kinsman Charles de Luxembourg, comte de Brienne
(1488–1530), as lieutenant-general of Picardy, a post he held until
1538. After Vendôme's death in 1537, François also temporarily
held the governorship until Antoine de Bourbon (1518–1562)
was eventually allowed to succeed his father as governor on
10 February 1538, the same day on which François was made full
governor of the Île-de-France and Anne de Montmorency was
appointed Constable of France (a post formerly held by the
deceased duc de Bourbon).[8]

There were other links to the king from the province through
Montmorency and the *chambre du roi*. Jean II d'Humières, whose
daughter Charlotte had married François de Montmorency in
1525, was by 1531 a *gentilhomme de la chambre*. Jean de Créquy, seigneur
de Canaples, was a champion jouster and a royal favourite. François
de Rasse, seigneur de La Hargerie, worked industriously supervising the administration of the province and was a *maître d'hôtel* in
the royal household from 1528.[9] Between them, these men and
their associates held the bulk of the captaincies of principal towns,
ports and fortifications, *baillages* (bailiwicks), and masterships of
waters and forests in the province, but never exercised a complete

Jean Clouet, *Anne de Montmorency, Connestable of France*, 1520s, chalk on paper.

monopoly on appointments over and against the nominees of
the duc de Vendôme. While most *gentilshommes* in the early 1530s
at least owed their places to prior family royal service and/or
Montmorency, there were also those who were preferred by Admiral
Chabot. A number of those were from families who were moving
into the orbit of Claude de Lorraine, duc de Guise, although his
family's influence in the household was not as strong under Francis
as it would be under Henri II.

These examples could be multiplied across the kingdom. That
is how Renaissance monarchy worked: through family and regional
connections between the great nobles holding important royal
offices, and local lower nobles holding local offices, whose English
counterparts would be called the gentry – the sheriffs, justices
of the peace and the like. Similar links were also maintained by
noble families with court connections, to members of city councils,
parlementaire families of lawyers and judges, and so on. The result
was that in the 1530s and '40s, under the king's aegis and control,
a network of contacts in the provinces below the level of the
great dukes and close royal friends was built up that had not existed
to quite the same extent, or in quite the same way, before 1525.
Whatever they later became, under Francis the *gentilshommes de la
chambre* were not ceremonial supernumeraries, but active agents
in enabling the king's writ to run as effectively as it apparently did.
They were one important means – albeit only one – by which
Francis secured the cooperation of powerful individuals and
through them that of wider interest groups within the French
polity.

SPACES AND PLACES FOR THE COURT:
FRANCIS'S ARCHITECTURAL PATRONAGE

The steadily increasing size of the court in the years after 1526 required larger accommodation and amenities, although Francis continued to maintain the tradition of the king himself having comparatively little personal space and 'living among his subjects'. This led, during the second half of the reign, to a near-constant programme of refurbishment of royal châteaux and the building of new ones. He created large residences for the whole court and smaller châteaux known as *maisons de plaisance* or *retrait*. In these residences there were no large public reception rooms, and the king could enjoy greater privacy with fewer, chosen companions. In all Francis's building and decoration, his personal love of the classical style, which had partly impelled his interest in Milan and all things Italian, remained the driving factor in design.

At his return from Spain, Francis was very conscious of the important roles, positive and negative, that the city and people of Paris had played in his kingdom during his absence. He promised to spend more time in Paris, partly to show his appreciation for its (albeit grudging) support, partly to establish closer personal and cultural ties between court and capital, and partly to supervise the *Parlement* and the university. His architectural patronage was therefore increasingly focused in the capital and the Île-de-France. He gave money for the building of a new Hôtel de Ville for Paris and offered a design by Domenico da Cortona (*c.* 1465– *c.* 1549), a pupil of the architect and military engineer Giuliano da Sangallo (*c.* 1445–1516), who was himself patronized by the Medici. The design was accepted by the municipal authorities. At the Louvre, Francis refurbished the accommodation for the queen and himself in the range that ran along the Seine, and included a suite of rooms adjacent to his own apartments for Anne de Montmorency. Towards the end of his reign, Francis also ordered the demolition of the west wing of the old Louvre

and the construction of what is now the southwest wing of the
Cour Carrée, although most of what we see in that space today was
the work of Henri II and subsequent patrons. It was used frequently, but the Louvre was never intended to be the principal
royal residence in or near the capital.[10]

To the west of Paris, Francis refurbished the château of
Saint-Germain-en-Laye. From the later 1530s onwards, he created much larger royal lodgings there than at the Louvre. The
area of the king's private *chambre* at Saint-Germain-en-Laye was
100 square metres (1,075 sq. ft), with views out over the garden,
the park and the river. These apartments were linked by bridges
to the park and from there to the hunting forest, which was one
of the king's favourites. The roof was also made into a spacious
terrace overlooking the forest. Not far from there, Francis built
the *maison de plaisance* La Muette, where he could spend time with
his close friends, special guests and his *petite bande* of ladies. In 1543
he was furious when two Italian lords unwittingly disturbed his
peace by presenting themselves there.[11]

Between the Louvre and Saint-Germain-en-Laye, within what
is now the Bois de Boulogne, Francis built an entirely new hunting
château, known as Madrid. It was almost certainly named after
the Casa del Campo, not far from the Alcázar of Madrid, which
Francis knew from his time in Spain, and from which the larger
building at Boulogne took direct inspiration. Work began in early
1528 on a rectangular structure with no courtyard or moat. The
central block contained a hall and public spaces on its three principal levels, and was flanked on either side by two square blocks of
reception rooms and 32 accommodation apartments. The principal
rooms on all levels gave out on to loggias with views across the
park. The external decoration of the château was in polychrome
glazed terracotta done under the direction of the Florentine
sculptor Girolamo della Robbia (1488–1566), whom Francis had
patronized since the late 1520s. The external decoration still

impressed the English gentleman traveller and diarist John Evelyn when he visited the château in February 1644.[12]

Francis's love of hunting found expression at Fontainebleau where the king renovated and extended an existing château, in order to give him access to the large hunting forests in the area. It soon became the residence in which he eventually took greatest pride, that he regarded as his home and where he spent more time than anywhere else apart from Paris. The design, probably by the king himself, was committed to his master mason Gilles le Breton (d. 1553), who began work in 1528. The first project was refurbishing an old castle, roughly oval in shape, that eventually became the heart of a much larger residence. Around the centre of the castle, the *Cour Ovale*, new lodgings were constructed for the royal family and close courtiers, together with a ballroom and galleries. The principal entrance to the restored château was a double-storeyed monumental gateway with open loggias, the *Porte Dorée*, inspired by that attributed to Luciano Laurana (*c.* 1420–1479) at the palace of the Montefeltro dukes in Urbino. A new wing was also begun at this time, which linked the king's lodgings to a nearby Trinitarian monastery to the west. The first floor housed what became known as the Galerie François Ier. After his mother's death in 1531, Francis took over her rooms within the royal apartments of the château and incorporated them, and the gallery, into an extended suite of lodgings for himself. The gallery itself was reserved for the king's private use, and he kept the key on his person. There is some evidence, although not conclusive, that the royal library was, for a time at least, housed on the floor above the gallery. The Orléans-Angoulême collection had first been moved from Cognac to Blois, where, in 1516, Federico Gonzaga had been shown over it by the king himself. Francis had wanted to guide his guest there one evening after dinner. On arriving, and finding the door locked and without the key, the king made to break it in with his shoulder – an example of his trust in his physical strength and sometimes alarming spontaneity. Federico begged the king not to risk injuring himself, and they saw it together the following day.[13] The library formed the basis of what eventually became the Bibliothèque Nationale de France, of which Francis is esteemed as founder.

Below the gallery at Fontainebleau, on the ground floor, a corridor connecting the château to the old monastery was enclosed, and here new royal baths were built, with cool, warm and hot rooms heated from furnaces and hypocausts below. New privy kitchens for the king were also built there, backing on to the baths and sharing the same heat source. Francis's conception of the palace as his main residence led to further building and decoration. A new monumental double staircase was also built in the *Cour Ovale* leading to the royal apartments.

The stables at Fontainebleau were enlarged, and Francis had new kennels built for his hunting dogs. The facilities southwest of Paris linked the area to the larger hunting forests in the Loire Valley. Thereafter Francis had royal forests stretching from his birthplace at Cognac, on the Charente, up through the Loire Valley and into the Île-de-France. As the Venetian ambassador Andrea Navagero (1483–1529), who died at Blois, reported:

Château of Fontainebleau.

Close to Blois there is a beautiful forest more than eleven leagues long and four wide, in which there are several houses of pleasure, built by different kings to allow them to hunt and to relax. It has a great number and variety of beasts; among them a deer whose horns are no less admirable than those of the one of which I spoke above. It is forbidden to hunt it for, in every respect, it is considered a real marvel.[14]

Breeding and exchanging horses, dogs and birds was common among noblemen and courtiers. For example, soon after his arrival at the French court as ambassador of Ercole II d'Este, Duke of Ferrara, in 1536, Cardinal Ippolito II d'Este (1509–1572), the duke's younger brother, received three deerhounds as a welcome gift. He wrote home later that year asking that his own dogs and falcons be sent to him. These included peregrines and sakers acquired in Ferrara and Venice. A peregrine could cost as much as 10 *scudi* (about 25 *livres tournois*).[15] Jean, Cardinal of Lorraine (of whom more later in this chapter), and his brother the duc de Lorraine promised to send some dogs to Duke Ercole. In January 1537 Ippolito sent him a few dogs, one of which he had seen run after 'a deer which I killed in the park at Vincennes, where it ran very well'. In the autumn of the following year Ercole also gave several lannerets to the king. 'He liked them very much,' Ippolito told his brother, 'and examined each one carefully.'[16]

Like his contemporary Henry VIII, Francis prided himself on his architectural patronage, and rarely missed an opportunity to show off his châteaux to ambassadors from England and elsewhere, as well as to his own courtiers. His patronage of painting and sculpture comfortably exceeded Henry's and more than rivalled that of Charles V. There is evidence that even before his accession, Francis was known to love painting. We have already noted the presence of Leonardo in his court from 1516, and

Leo x's gift of the *St Michael* by Raphael in 1518. John Evelyn called
Francis 'that great virtuoso' and noted that the king had been so
impressed by Leonardo's fresco of the Last Supper in Santa Maria
delle Grazie, Milan, that he had investigated the possibility of
detaching it and taking it back to France with him.[17] In 1516 the
Florentine painter Andrea del Sarto (1486–1530) also spent time
at the French court. Francis commissioned several works from
him but only one, the painting *Charity* (1518/19), now in the Louvre,
is known to have been completed.

The artists whom Francis patronized more than any others
in the earlier part of his reign were, however, not Italian, but
Flemish: Jean Clouet (*c.* 1485–*c.* 1540/41) and his son François
(*c.* 1515/20–1572). Alongside Jean Bourdichon (1457/9–1521)
and Jean Perréal (*c.* 1455/60–1530), the elder Clouet had worked
for Louis XII, and became a retained royal artist in 1516. He was
also a skilled miniaturist and produced the portraits of Francis's
generals at Marignano that illustrated François Demoulins's *Les
Commentaires de la guerre gallique*.

Jean Clouet became principal court painter and a *valet de chambre*
to Francis. He made many portraits in chalk, charcoal and oil of
the members of the French court, including one of the king's
sister Marguerite holding a parrot. He also painted the best-known
portrait of the king, made in 1526 (see Chapter Two), probably to
record and celebrate his return from captivity in Spain. Now in
the Louvre, the painting shows the king seated in three-quarter
profile, resting his right arm on a parapet covered in green velour.
He is dressed in a sumptuous silk doublet in a variation of his
personal livery colours of white, tawny and black. Its cut emphasizes – indeed exaggerates – the width of Francis's shoulders and
accentuates his bare neck, around which he wears the lesser collar
of the Order of Saint-Michel. The king's left hand rests on the
pommel of a dagger and his right hand lightly holds a pair of fine
leather gloves.[18] As was by then the fashion, it is an image that

Titian, *Francis I, c.* 1538, oil on canvas.

emphasizes his personal qualities as the first gentleman of France, rather than his formal status as monarch.

The essential elements of the Clouet composition are also found in the only portrait of the king to equal, and perhaps eclipse, that of 1526. In 1538 Titian (1488/90–1576) made a portrait of Francis in profile, now also in the Louvre. It was presented to the king that year by the Venetian humanist writer and collector Pietro Aretino (1492–1556) in the hope of securing work as the king's agent in Italy. The painting shows to the full Titian's genius in the use of chiaroscuro, the technique of light and shade. The light focuses attention on the king's face and neck, as does Clouet's portrait, but is here framed in shadow by his upper body and wide shoulders. This darkness, in turn, enhances the contrasting sheen of the king's satin doublet, which is slightly parted down the centre of the chest, and the slashes or cuts in the sleeves through which the fabric of his shirt is fashionably plucked and tied. The brilliant whiteness of the shirt shines out of these partings, as an inner light radiating from Francis's body beneath. It illuminates the medal of the lesser collar of the Order of Saint-Michel that the king wears, and also catches the badge and the white ostrich plume at the brim of his hat. His gloved hand rests on the pommel of a dagger, as in Clouet's 1526 painting.[19]

Francis's portraits, and the *argenterie* and *chambre aux deniers* accounts for his jewels, clothing and other accoutrements, show that his patronage encompassed a wide range of creative endeavour beyond architecture and painting. It included the tailors, embroiders, milliners and shoemakers who fashioned his apparel, the bowmakers and armourers who made his hunting and jousting equipment, and those who made the instruments for the music that entertained him and his guests. Francis invested heavily in tapestries, which were useful as insulation and as colourful and costly wall decoration. He never possessed anything like the more than 2,500 tapestries and hangings reputedly owned by Henry of England, but Francis may have had about 1,500 pieces, which were looked after by Guillaume Moynier, his principal *tappisier*. They included an ornate set of 23 pieces of the story of Scipio purchased in 1532 for use at the meeting with Henry in October that year (see Chapter Four) at a cost of 50,000 *livres*. Francis had also bought tapestries twelve years earlier for his accommodation at Ardres for the Field of Cloth of Gold.[20]

Francis also patronized gold- and silversmiths, many of them Parisian, for everything from utensils and talking-pieces for the royal tables to the adornments on his clothing, the jewellery he wore, and the vessel, plate and collars given as gifts to other princes, to their ambassadors and to his own noble servants and friends. Apart from Benvenuto Cellini (of whom more later in this chapter), the most prominent were Jean Hotman and Pierre Mangot (both *fl.* 1520s–40s). These two craftsmen furnished the king with hundreds of items, including diplomatic gifts and an exquisite coffer (now in the collection of the Earl of Chesterfield) that, in itself, demonstrates the remarkable skill and ingenuity Francis had at his command. The king seems to have had an early form of cabinet of curiosities on an attic floor above his apartments at Fontainebleau, and there his private collection of ancient medals, silverware, jewels and figurines was displayed.[21]

FINANCIAL RESOURCES AND REFORMS

All this artistic patronage did not come cheap. Nor did the wars and diplomacy of Francis's early reign, which were astronomically expensive. The 1515 Marignano campaign alone had cost some 7.5 million *livres tournois*, and the 'Perpetual Peace' of Fribourg, securing the future services of Swiss mercenaries, a further million. To this had been added the comparatively modest cost of the return of Tournai in 1518, the annual pensions paid to Henry and a large number of English and some imperial courtiers, and the 400,000 *livres* Francis is estimated to have spent on the Field of Cloth of Gold. These were as nothing, however, when compared to the cost of war between 1521 and 1524, which has been estimated at a staggering 20 million *livres*.[22]

Unsurprisingly, there was a huge crown deficit even by the early 1520s, and Francis had a pressing need both to increase royal income and to ensure receipt of revenues that he was owed. He had inherited from his predecessors a ramshackle fiscal adminis-tration based on the traditional distinction between 'ordinary' and 'extraordinary' revenue. The king's 'ordinary' revenue came from the crown's estates and alienated lands, from customs, from the profits of justice and from *venalité* – the sale of noble titles and royal judicial and fiscal offices for profit. Francis was not the first king to adopt this expedient, but he did so on a much larger scale than any of his predecessors, and with important consequences for his successors. Four *trésoriers de France* were responsible for the collection and disbursement of this revenue.

The king's 'extraordinary' revenue came predominantly from taxes and was to be used mainly for warfare and defence. The principal royal tax was the *taille*: the *taille réelle*, which was payable by all people in a minority of regions of the kingdom; and the *taille personelle*, which fell on commoners across the majority of provinces. The clergy, the nobility and a range of other social or professional groups and some major towns were exempted. These imposts together were the single most profitable tax source for the crown. Income from them doubled during Francis's reign, from 2.4 million *livres* per annum in 1515 to 4.6 million in 1544–5.[23] There was also indirect taxation, upon which Francis relied heavily. Dues and sales taxes, called *aides*, were payable on a range of goods and were levied principally in the towns, where markets were part of daily life. These dues were usually resisted, and some provinces, includ-ing Burgundy and Provence, were exempt. Perhaps the most famous sales tax was the *gabelle*, on salt. At their height, *gabelle* revenues under Francis reached 700,000 *livres* per annum.

Francis did not generally add to these forms of taxation, but in 1543 he extended the scope of one tax, the *solde de gens*, to raise troops. The overall sums collected by these various forms of indirect taxation were comparatively small at about 1.6 million *livres* in 1515, which had risen to 2.8 million by 1547. A very high proportion of this money never reached the treasury but was assigned in the localities. The Church was also subject to royal taxation. The *décime* or tenth was levied in times of emergency and, theoretically, only with papal approval. Over the course of his reign, Francis levied 57 tenths, of which only a tiny minority were papally sanctioned, with an estimated total yield of around 18 million *livres*.[24]

Non-clerical taxation revenue was administered by four *généraux des finances*. Each was responsible for a *généralité*, itself divided into *élections* in which officials called *élus* operated. They sat alongside the four *trésoriers de France* responsible for 'ordinary' revenue (see above). These two groups of officials were wealthy, often related to each other and known collectively as the *gens de finance*. The cumbersome system of collecting revenues and paying crown debts by assignments gave ample scope for evasion and embezzlement. Consequently, there was routinely a wide discrepancy between what the crown was owed and what it actually collected. Francis was therefore obliged to raise money from voluntary and forced loans from wealthy individuals, from towns, from French and foreign bankers, and from his own financial officials. There was a more or less permanent recourse to loans throughout his reign, with varying rates of interest and lengths of repayment for each.

Even before his second Italian war, the king realized that this complex fiscal administration needed reform, and this was reinforced by the military setbacks of 1521. In the two years that followed he used every expedient that came to hand, from selling more crown offices to alienating its lands and exhausting his credit with all his bankers. In January 1523 he established a special commission to investigate malfeasance, and this became a wider effort at reforming the financial system. A number of his leading financial officials were investigated, and in March a new central financial official was appointed, the *Trésorier de l'Épargne*. He was to be responsible for revenues from the king's royal domains and from taxation. Another treasurer, the receiver of the *parties casuelles*, supervised all other sources of income, from loans to sales of royal offices. These appointments were made to increase the king's direct control of his finances, thereby ensuring he had ready cash to hand, in a kind of current account whose funds he could readily measure and out of which he paid his immediate expenses. The *Épargne* did not in fact receive all the revenues intended for it, but it did improve their collection significantly.[25]

When Francis returned from Spain, he referred the records of his financiers to a court of auditors, the *Chambre des Comptes*, and established another special financial commission, the *Tour Carrée*, which investigated financial fraud. Its most conspicuous detainee was Jacques de Beaune, baron de Semblançay (1445/65–1527), a very wealthy former member of the king's financial council, to whom Francis owed almost 2 million *livres* from outstanding loans and charges. Beaune had acted as the king's personal financier, and that for Louise de Savoie, in addition to his formal duties. Therein lay his downfall. He was charged with misappropriating crown funds, something of which he had been accused in 1523 but finally cleared in 1525. Now, despite little if any new evidence and without the assistance of those in a position to verify the truth, he was found guilty and sentenced to death. Although many expected the king would pardon him, he was hanged on 12 August 1527.[26] It was thought at the time and since that this was unduly harsh. The court poet Clément Marot (*c.* 1496–1544) wrote a reflective octave on his death. The execution seems to have been less about punishing actual wrongdoing than about setting an example to other officials – and, just possibly, freeing the king from significant debts.

Over the course of the following decade, further reforms along the lines laid out in 1523 were initiated, such as those under the Edict of Rouen (1532), whereby all royal revenue apart from that from the *parties casuelles* was to be paid into the treasury of the *Épargne*. Against the background of continuing war with Charles, the financial reform process continued in the last decade of Francis's reign. It proceeded not from any far-sighted revision of the fiscal administration as such, but from desperate necessity. These reforms culminated with the Edict of Cognac in 1542, when the *Épargne* became the core of a tighter and *comparatively* more efficient financial administration.

'SUPREME HEAD'? FRANCIS AND THE FRENCH CHURCH

Francis was a patron in the widest sense of the term, and his view of that patronage was at one with his pronounced sense of authority as king. He asserted direct control over as many aspects of the governing and well-being of his kingdom as he could, not least its finances and administration. A similar vigour characterized his approach to the Church and religion within the realm generally. Unlike his great rival Henry of England, however, Francis felt no need to break with Rome in order to assert his authority over the Church. He was as appalled by Henry's schism as any other Catholic monarch and, formally at least, favoured a reconciliation. Yet, doctrinally orthodox as he was, Francis was less conventional in his approach to questions of faith and of the Church hierarchy than many of his Catholic contemporaries. He may never have fundamentally contested papal authority in France as such, but he insisted that it operated under royal supervision. He directed and limited its reach at every turn. It is at least arguable that in so doing – and in maintaining a close personal supervision of senior ecclesiastical appointments, while also taxing its resources to the full – Francis made himself the de facto 'supreme head' of the Church in France.

As we have seen, the Concordat of Bologna in 1516 had increased, rather than otherwise, the crown's effective control of senior ecclesiastical appointments. Francis used this patronage to the full, ensuring that in most cases his preferred candidates obtained senior vacancies, such as abbacies and bishoprics, even if they were formally presented to their positions by the pope. Papal imposts, such as annates, continued to be paid, while Francis also taxed the Church heavily for his own purposes. The majority of appointees at the highest levels were men from noble families whose commitment to their ecclesiastical duties varied. Perhaps the most famous of them was Jean, Cardinal of Lorraine (1498– 1550). He was the younger brother of Antoine, duc de Lorraine, and first met Francis at his brother's wedding in June 1515. Three years later, at the age of twenty, he was made a cardinal. He was present at the Field of Cloth of Gold and, according to some sources at least, accompanied the king on his campaign in 1524–5, but escaped after Pavia unharmed. Lorraine was always more a courtier than a committed churchman, and played a key role in receiving and entertaining the king's guests. Others, such as Antoine Duprat and François de Tournon, were, in the continuing medieval tradition, more administrators and royal agents than working ecclesiastics. Another such was Claude de Seyssel, the author, as noted earlier, of *La Monarchie de France*. He was bishop, first of Marseilles and then, from 1517 until his death in 1520, of Turin.

When it came to bishops who worked mainly in their dioceses, Francis was fortunate in the quality of the episcopate he inherited from Louis. Among the most prominent of them were François d'Estaing of Rodez (in post 1504–29), Guillaume Briçonnet, bishop of Meaux (1470–1534), Jacques Lefèvre d'Étaples (*c.* 1455–1536) and Étienne Poncher (1446–1524), the last of whom was successively bishop of Paris and archbishop of Sens. This group worked to eradicate abuses in the Church, remedying problems of vacancies and pluralism and setting examples of good pastoral supervision of their dioceses, visiting parishes and monastic houses regularly. They also promoted high standards of morality and preaching among parish priests. Francis allowed this group of prelates a remarkable degree of freedom in discussion and debate about desirable reforms, and many of them enjoyed the support of Louise de Savoie and Marguerite de Navarre.[27]

Yet even this narrowly licensed debate alarmed the more conservative elements in the Church, who were supported by the Faculty of Theology at the University of Paris. The Sorbonne criticized much reformist debate in the mid-1520s as tending towards heresy. It was in turn supported by the *Parlement* of Paris, which enforced laws on heresy as on other matters. Francis understood this resistance to novel ideas perfectly well, and he never contested their roles in identifying and combating heresy as such, but it was as much a matter of interpretation as anything else. In the early period of what became the Reformation, the lines between legitimate debate about reform and heretical thought were not always easy to draw. The king saw the licence for discussion he gave as an expression of his royal authority and resented the implication that in granting it, he was tolerating heresy. Francis was determined that he would not finally be told what to think by either the university or the *Parlement*.

The careful line Francis saw himself as treading – between allowing legitimate debate about theological truth and clerical reform, and defending orthodoxy and fighting heresy – was tested frequently and not always maintained successfully. He and Louise, as regent during his absence in Italy and Spain, clashed

several times with the faculty and with the *Parlement*, intervening
to protect such prominent evangelical thinkers as Gérard Roussel,
Louis de Berquin, Guillaume Cop and Briçonnet from accusations
of heresy. This more nuanced position was challenged as never
before by the Affair of the Placards in October 1534, a series of
attacks on the Mass itself, and particularly the doctrine of tran-
substantiation, mounted by a group of radical evangelicals. One
Sunday, posters or 'placards' using alarming and abusive language
to attack the central sacrament of the Catholic faith appeared in
Paris, in several provincial towns and even at the royal château of
Amboise. They caused outrage and panic about violent extremism
in equal measure. Things had gone far enough – too far, it seemed.
The universities and the regional *parlements* of the realm looked
to the king to demonstrate his credentials as an effective governor
and defender of the Church.

In this febrile climate, the king's room for manoeuvre was
very limited, and he responded to the affair as being as much a
challenge to his royal authority as an unacceptable attack on
orthodoxy. Francis ordered a crackdown on those responsible and
on Lutheran sympathies more generally. Thereafter, and even as
he began negotiating with Lutheran princes for military alliances
against Charles v, the king took a much stricter line on Lutherans
within France itself. In defending his reputation as a religious
monarch, he assiduously attacked heretical threats of any sort. For
example, he countenanced the repression by authorities in Provence
not of Lutherans, but of the Waldensians or Vaudois, a dissent-
ing community established in southern France long before the
Reformation. Action against them was prompted as much by local
political and cultural hostility as by fear of active heterodoxy, but
Francis sanctioned brutal repression that might well be described
today as ethnic cleansing.[28]

SECOND MARRIAGE AND FURTHER PATRONAGE

Not long before his mother's last illness, Francis had married for the second time. His betrothal to Eleanor of Portugal had been part of the Treaty of Madrid in 1526. They had first met in the Spanish city and had been married by proxy but, as we have seen, were not finally married until Eleanor came to France in July 1530. She made her formal entry to Paris after her coronation at Saint-Denis on 5 March the following year. Brantôme said of the queen that 'when dressed, she seemed a very beautiful princess,' before rather ungallantly implying that it was a different story when she was unclothed. Francis made it plain from the outset that he had no love for his new queen and had no need of further heirs from her. In 1533 his sister giggled with the Duke of Norfolk, then Henry's ambassador in France, about Eleanor's evident desire 'to be too much embraced' by her husband, even though she was 'not pleasant to his appetite'.[29] Nor did Francis require his wife's help, either in the conduct of his foreign relations or in the great cultural projects that absorbed his energies in the years after they married.

Eleanor had some hopes of increased importance when the dauphin François was betrothed to Marie of Portugal, her daughter by her first marriage. These came to nothing, however, with the dauphin's death in 1536. Two years later she supported plans for the king's youngest son, Charles d'Orléans, to be married to her niece and his being eventually invested with the duchy of Milan, in order to settle the long-running Valois–Habsburg conflict. She was prominent when her brother visited France in late 1539, but when, early the next year, Charles defied the French again over Milan, such influence as the queen may have acquired was lost entirely. Her revived hopes of the Milan settlement, as the basis of the Peace of Crépy in 1544 (see Chapter Four), saw her make a tour of the Netherlands with the young duc d'Orléans, but his death in September the following year ended those hopes.

Eleanor thus remained a marginal figure at the French court, and she left France as soon as she politely could after her husband's death. She went first to Brussels, then (with her younger sister, Mary of Hungary) accompanied their brother to Spain in 1556. She and Mary settled near Charles at Jarandilla de la Vera in Extremadura. Eleanor died in February 1558, Charles in September and Mary in October the same year.

Eleanor had arrived in France at the same time as Francis's two eldest sons returned from Spain. François, now aged twelve, and Henri, eleven, together with their three younger siblings, had their own accommodation and entourages under the overall supervision of Montmorency. Their education, like their father's, was in the fashionable humanities, and the two elder princes had been accompanied throughout their time in Spain (even after the majority of their entourages had been dismissed in January 1528) by a tutor, the Genoese humanist Benedetto Tagliacarne (*c.* 1480–1536). Probably originally recruited by secretary Robertet, and known in France as Benoit Théocréne, he was made bishop of Grasse in 1534. Marot, whose own fame was at its height at this time under Francis's patronage, dedicated a slightly tongue-in-cheek rondeau to Théocréne in his collection *l'Adolescence Clémentine* (1532). The education of the younger royal children, meanwhile, was supervised by another humanist poet, Mellin de Saint-Gelais (1490/91–1558).[30]

Francis's indifferent courtesy to his wife was, from the outset, in contrast to his public adoration of the woman who became the most important at his court during the second half of his reign: Anne de Pisseleu, dame d'Heilly (1508–*c.* 1580). Francis had met this unmarried daughter of an impoverished nobleman immediately upon his return to France, and apparently at his mother's suggestion. Anne had evidently impressed Louise enough at their introduction to be taken into her household, and she was one of Louise's ladies-in-waiting at her reunion with her son at

Bordeaux. The king was immediately captivated by Anne, and she returned with him to Paris, where he flaunted her before the court and the city. As the English ambassador Sir Francis Bryan reported on the day of the queen's coronation, Francis had Anne 'set before him in an open window and there stood devising [chatting] with her two long hours in the sight and face of all the people'.[31] Anne's appearance in 1526 spelled the end for Madame de Châteaubriant, who was then at home in Brittany, daily expecting the call to resume her place at the king's side. It never came. She plied him with poetry, which they had always enjoyed together, but to no unavail. Francis was politely solicitous in the way former lovers can sometimes be, but indifferent now to her. He stayed with her and her husband, Jean de Laval, on his tour of Brittany in 1531 and made Jean the governor of the province that year. Allegations of her husband's cruelty towards Françoise continued, and she died in October 1537, aged 43.

Although physically different – blonde and blue-eyed – from the brunette Françoise, Anne had many of the qualities that Francis had admired in his first mistress. Personally charming and witty, she was also intelligent and evidently learned, despite her relatively straitened circumstances as a child. She was a keen athlete, riding and swimming for exercise. After Louise's death, in 1531, Anne became the king's acknowledged mistress and the governess of his daughters, and she formed an early friendship with Marguerite de Navarre. Anne's humble familial status nevertheless presented a problem for Francis, one that he solved by having her marry his friend Jean IV de Brosse, comte de Penthièvre (1505–1565), in 1534. Two years later Francis made Jean duc d'Étampes, and it is as Madame d'Étampes that Anne is known to history. The king enjoyed the company of gentlewomen and, as Brantôme noted in the 1570s, had his 'petite bande' of women – apart from his formal mistresses – who accompanied him when he travelled and hunted. After the chase Francis would, reportedly, rest or take

further exertion with some one or more of the ladies. Brantôme quotes him as saying, 'for in truth a court without ladies is like a garden without flowers' – probably the single phrase for which Francis is best known. With some of these women Francis was, doubtless, sexually involved at different times, but the impression given by later historians, chiefly Jules Michelet in the nineteenth century, that they formed some sort of harem was wide of the mark.[32]

Corneille de Lyon (attrib.), *Anne de Pisseleu, Duchesse d'Étampes, c.* 1535–40, oil on wood.

As is the case for virtually every royal mistress, 'la belle Heilly' quickly became a controversial figure. Her supporters saw in her the same qualities as did the king. For her detractors, she always remained a bumpkin upstart, despite her accomplishments, her material greed matched only by her capacity to involve herself in matters of state at the highest level. Anne was indeed enriched by the king both directly and through her husband's income. She established an *hôtel particulier* in Paris and acquired a number of châteaux, including Challau in the Île-de-France, which Francis gave to her in 1545. She shared his enjoyment of architecture and painting, and patronized artists including Francesco Primaticcio (1504–1570).

Foremost among Madame d'Étampes' critics were Anne de Montmorency and Henri d'Orléans, together with the latter's wife, Catherine de' Medici, and his mistress Diane de Poitiers (*c.* 1500–1566). For the remainder of the king's reign, they and their supporters formed a group against whom Anne chose, or was forced, to position herself. The rivals to that group, among them the dauphin François and Admiral Chabot and their clients, watched her growing influence with the king and sought to bring her into their circle. Consequently, Anne became a social and political patron in her own right, rather as Anne Boleyn was in England in the late 1520s, during the years of her 'unofficial' relationship with Henry VIII. These oppositional parties, or factions, became more entrenched after the dauphin's death in 1536, when Anne allied with the king's youngest son, Charles, now duc d'Orléans. The lines of allegiance were largely maintained until Charles's death in 1545, with, as we shall see, important consequences for the conduct of diplomacy and warfare in Francis's ongoing battles with Charles V.

The decade of Anne's ascendancy from 1531 saw the court expand to its fullest extent and with it the king's most important architectural and artistic patronage, on which he spent more money than anything other than warfare. The building works outlined above, at the Louvre, at Saint-Germain-en-Laye and at the Bois de Boulogne, were completed. At Fontainebleau, the programme of works continued through the 1530s. The numerous changes and additions made to the palace by rulers as recent as Napoleon mean that the Galerie François 1er is now the only space at Fontainebleau that can still be associated directly with the king. The gallery is likely to have been completed by the end of 1539. The panelling on its lower walls, featuring Francis's 'F' *chiffre* and his salamanders, was done by Francesco Scibec da Carpi (*fl.* before 1559). Above it, the decoration was carried out under the super-vision of the Florentine artist Giovanni Battista di Jacopo, known as Rosso Fiorentino (1494–1540), who was recommended to Francis by the Venetian agent Aretino. Rosso's frescoes were set within elaborate stucco frames featuring nudes, garlands of flowers and crops, swags, fruit and strapwork. The style of Florentine mannerism, sometimes also called the First School of Fontainebleau, is evident in the François gallery, which has been much altered in appearance over the centuries. According to Vasari in his *Lives of the Artists*, Francis was immediately impressed with the work and enjoyed Rosso's company, for he 'was a large man with red hair corresponding to his name, and in all his actions, he was serious, considerate, and very judicious'.[33]

The gallery was 'restored' in the mid-nineteenth century and again in the 1960s, and has been intensively studied since. The outcome of this research is the current understanding that its iconographic programme presents a range of classical settings that allude to Francis's kingship. Populated by nymphs and youths, gods and goddesses – all idealized forms of the human body – the frescoes present elements of well-known, as well as more arcane, episodes from Graeco-Roman history and mythology. Many depict opposing qualities, vices and virtues, such as lust and love, peace and war, ignorance and learning. Most refer to Francis allegorically as an imperial ruler who, by his intelligence and wisdom, his governance of the realm and his patronage of the arts and learning, shows the way forward, or resolves the oppositional forces depicted in the settings. Some frescoes may allude to episodes in Francis's reign, as well as to his sons' filial piety to him and his own towards his mother. Vasari, who never saw the scheme, was rightly informed that it made some allusions to the life of Alexander the Great. A full articulation of the decorative programme still eludes scholars, however, and it may only ever have been known to the king himself, who could explain it confidentially to his guests. Overall, its decoration (and indeed most throughout the palace) made the less-than-subtle point that, whatever the Habsburg ruler's formal title, it was Francis who was the true inheritor and best appreciator of the beauty and philosophy of the ancient world – and that he was the *real* emperor. That had been the message of *Les Commentaires de la guerre gallique* after Marignano, and now it was painted more vividly still on the walls of the gallery at Fontainebleau.[34]

To the west of the main residence, built on the lands of the former Trinitarian monastery and at right angles to the wing containing the gallery, Francis set out an autonomous building that he called the 'château neuf'. From 1539 this range itself became the foundation of a new base, or outer, court eventually known as the Cour de Cheval Blanc because a plaster cast of the equestrian statue of Marcus Aurelius later stood there.[35] New wings were begun to the north and south for the accommodation and entertainment of the court. The south wing overlooked the gardens and the pond, and its decoration was carried out from designs by Francesco Primaticcio. He had developed his skills in painting and stucco-moulding while apprenticed to Giulio Romano (1492/9–1546) at the Gonzaga court in Mantua. These he first deployed during the last decade of Francis's reign, designing the decorations for the king's and queen's bedchambers, and those of

Madame d'Étampes. He was also responsible for the decoration of the ballroom and the Galerie d'Ulysse on the first floor of the south wing of the square court. Most of its 58 scenes (which took more than fifty years to complete) illustrate episodes from the *Odyssey* and the *Iliad*. It may have taken its inspiration from the king's love of Greek literature, as in the Galerie François Ier, but this much larger and longer space was only begun in about 1546, shortly before Francis's death. It introduced the second style, or school, of Fontainebleau mannerism, with its elongated human forms and elaborate decorative features.[36]

    Equally expressive in its own way of Francis's imperial ambition was the château of Chambord, probably the one now most popularly associated with him alone. Newly built from the early years of his reign, but not completed until the second half, it gave

Rosso Fiorentino, *Venus Scolding Cupid*, 1535–40, fresco, Galerie François Ier, Fontainebleau.

Francis a magnificent hospitality venue in the forests of the Loire Valley, where he loved to hunt. Although the ground plan is medieval, essentially a towered keep flanked on three sides by protective ranges and towers set within a moat, the elevation is thoroughly Renaissance in spirit and design. Claims for Leonardo da Vinci as its designer have been made, so radically new was it in the French context, and because its most striking internal feature, the famous double-spiral staircase in the keep, resembles a design known to have been by him. This feature more bemused than impressed John Evelyn when he saw it in 1644, but he thought the chimneys of Chambord charming and 'like so many towers'. Domenico da Cortona has also been suggested as architect. He did make a model of Chambord in the 1530s, and had worked elsewhere for Francis, but no definite identification can be made for either Italian master. Whoever designed it, the French masons who worked on Chambord certainly showed a command of monumental symmetry and Italianate decorative features, such as volutes and cupolas, adapting them to a French context with those chimneys and high dormer roofs over the towers. The noted architect

Israël Silvestre, *Château de Chambord*, 1678, engraving.

Jacques I Androuet du Cerceau (1510/12?–1585) praised its scale and sophistication and the magnificent prospect it offered its visitors. This view was evidently shared by Louis XIV, who considered Chambord a palace for entertainment and spectacle second only to Versailles.[37]

Beyond the architects, builders and painters who decorated his palaces, Francis continued to patronize a wide range of artistic and intellectual endeavour during the second half of his reign. Sculptural skill was very largely concentrated in the Italian states at the time. One of the first sculptures Francis owned was a gift from Cardinal Ippolito d'Este, a copy of the famous ancient bronze of a boy pulling a thorn from his foot, known as *il Spinario*, which was for a long time located at Fontainebleau.[38] It was principally from Rome, Florence and Naples that Francis then obtained sculptures, or casts of them, to display at Fontainebleau and other châteaux. In this endeavour, he first turned to the art agent Giovanni Battista della Palla (1489–1532). The latter's correspondence with friends, among them the banker Filippo Strozzi (1489–1538), indicates that he knew Francis wished him to concentrate on obtaining the finest available antiquities, but the exact number of pieces he acquired for the king remains uncertain.[39] In 1540 and 1545 Francis decided to act directly, sending Primaticcio to Rome to make drawings of medals, triumphal arches, busts and other antiquities there. After Rosso's death at Fontainebleau in November 1540, Primaticcio had become the director of the decorative programme there, and on both visits to Rome, he bought numerous objects and made casts of bronzes. These were shipped to France, including one of the equestrian statue of Marcus Aurelius, the original of which is now in the Capitoline Museum. Payment records survive for as many as 133 cases of objects received at Fontainebleau. The casts were then used in a foundry near the château to produce copies of, among others, the *Apollo Belvedere*, *Sleeping Ariadne*, *Mercury* and the *Laocoön*. A copy of Michelangelo's *Hercules* was placed at the centre of what became the Cour de la Fontaine, and could be viewed from the Galerie François 1er.

Francis also wanted sculptors to come to France. The most famous artist to accept such an invitation was the Florentine Benvenuto Cellini (1500–1571). He had first met Francis in 1537 on a visit to France, but illness forced him to return home. From this period dates the famous medal of Francis 1 in the style of a Roman emperor, now in the Fitzwilliam Museum in Cambridge. After various scrapes and time in a papal prison in Rome – from which he was released at Francis's request and with the assistance of Cardinal d'Este – Cellini returned to France in September 1540, bringing a basin and ewer as gifts for his new patron. He was soon commissioned by Francis to create twelve silver candelabras of Olympian gods and goddesses, to be set around the royal table. After four years he had completed only one, the *Jupiter*, which he presented to the king in a dramatic manner in the Galerie François 1er in January 1544; the work has not survived. Cellini also made a number of other large works in bronze, including the *Nymph of Fontainebleau*, which celebrated the area as a hunting forest, and which is now in the Louvre. By 1545 Cellini had also completed a model for a huge statue of Mars, an allegorical figure of Francis himself as warrior king, in a style perhaps somewhat akin to his famous statue of *Perseus*, made later in Florence. First suggested in 1542, it was intended to be some 16.5 metres (54 ft) tall and set in a fountain at the château, with supporting figures alluding to Francis's patronage of arts and science, but the statue was never completed.

The most extraordinary creation that Cellini made for Francis and that has survived dates from 1543. This is the salt cellar now in the Kunsthistorisches Museum in Vienna (stolen in 2003 but since recovered). Fashioned of richly ornamented gold and silver, it features figures of Earth and the Ocean, with a hippocampus

and other sea creatures. It delighted Francis when it was first presented to him, but by 1545 the king had begun to lose patience with Cellini. Irascible, often violent and prone to petty jealousies (especially of Primaticcio), Cellini was difficult to deal with, even for the king. Despite being amply rewarded and granted French naturalization in an effort to keep him there permanently, Cellini left the court abruptly in July 1545, never to return. He did, nevertheless, in his famous autobiography credit Francis with giving him the means to be 'in part immortal, since the French king set me on the path of sculpture'.[40]

Jean Clouet, *Guillaume Budé, c.* 1536, oil on wood.

The fact that much of the decoration and sculptures acquired for Fontainebleau were of Greek subjects in part reflects Francis's increasing enthusiasm in the late 1530s for the study of that language. He began assiduously collecting Greek manuscripts and having translations of key texts made for himself, for circulation among his nobles at court, in accordance with a wish expressed as early as 1527 that 'we have always specially sought the training and education of all our good subjects, especially those who constitute the condition of nobility.'[41] Greek had an exotic allure and prestige that even the newly augmented humanist Latin lacked, being the mundane language of the Church, education and the law. An earlier generation of royal scholars, such as Guillaume Budé, had promoted the study of Greek, which the king supported, gradually but sincerely. One of the best-known images of Francis, now in the Musée Condé at Chantilly, is a miniature painting of the Greek specialist Antoine Macault reading to the court his translation of Diodorus of Sicily's *Universal History*. The miniature depicts the king seated at a table, surrounded by his three sons and close courtiers (both lay and ecclesiastical), listening to Macault.[42]

Throughout the last decade of his reign, Francis continued to patronize the work of humanist scholars. In 1530, urged on by Budé, who had published *Commentarii linguae graecae* (Commentaries on the Greek Language) the previous year, Francis endorsed the study of classical languages as essential to the proper understanding of scripture. He established four professorships, the *lecteurs royaux*, two in Greek and two in Hebrew. They formed the core of what later became the Collège de France, but there were problems with appointments and pay, and the scheme did not immediately improve the status of such learning within academia as the king intended it should. Among the first of these professors was Pierre du Chastel (*c.* 1480–1552), one of the king's chaplains, who sought Greek manuscripts for Francis from a variety of sources and offered him translations of others. When Chastel became *lecteur* in 1537, the royal library had forty Greek manuscripts. By 1544 it contained 270, and by the time of his death in 1552, it had 557 manuscripts and about 100 Greek books.

Francis was interested in Greek not simply for its own sake, but for its potential as a source of ideals with which to associate his kingship. One of the court's leading humanists, Hugues Salel (*c.* 1504–1553), a *valet de chambre* in the royal household, produced a French translation of Homer's *Iliad*, printed in the 1540s in a very chic folio volume with eleven woodcut illustrations. The French monarchy had long since been ascribed Trojan origins, but in his translation Salel began a trend towards identifying France more with the victorious Greeks, associating Francis with the warrior-king Agamemnon, who led them in battle. His translation of the *Iliad*, richly illustrated with exciting (if anachronistic) battle scenes, with horses and dogs, was intended primarily for the young noblemen who were still generally sent to court to complete their formal education – the sort of young men for whom Blaise de Monluc would later write his *Commentaires* on his military experience. Homer in French was designed to capture their imagination and focus it on a king who, although now ageing himself, had first proved his status as warrior counterpart to the Homeric heroes on the battlefield in his youth. The word *gentilhomme*, to which Francis had given renewed currency in the first days of his reign with the creation of the office of *gentilhomme de la chambre*, was still strongly associated with leading troops. Its root, *gens/gentliz*, meant 'noble, warrior-like'. According to Brantôme, Francis generally referred to himself as the *premier gentilhomme* of France, more than as its king.

Yet there was even more to Francis's interest in Greek than enhancing his reputation as a soldier and patron of learning among his courtiers. The king (or at least his scholars) also saw it as the best means to associate him with the development of

French itself. His own name was nearly synonymous with that
of the kingdom and its native tongue. Of course, there was no
one universal French language in the sixteenth century, but even
the two main forms still lacked coherence and even sufficient
technical words and abstract nouns, with which Greek was replete,
compared to Italian, German and even English. (The last of these
was undergoing its own period of dynamic growth in scope at
the time.) Francis sponsored efforts to improve and augment
the French language, to give it the facility of Greek and to have it
used in public contexts. These culminated in the Edict of Villers-
Cotterêts of 1539, which made French, not Latin, the language of
legal documents, although it took a long time for the edict to
become effective. Its spirit is summarized in clause III:

> And because so many things often hinge on the meaning
> of Latin words contained in the said documents, We will
> that from henceforth all decrees together with all other
> proceedings, whether of our royal courts or others sub-
> ordinate or inferior, whether records, surveys, contracts,
> commissions, awards, wills, and all other acts and deeds
> of justice or dependent thereon be spoken, written, and
> given to the parties in the French mother tongue and not
> otherwise.[43]

Francis's patronage of Greek scholarship was key to the later
vogue for French poetry and prose, informed by classical literature
more generally and championed by Pierre de Ronsard (1524–
1585), Joachim du Bellay (c. 1522–1560) and their circle, known
as La Pléiade.[44]

FOUR

The Warrior Again

All such as bear arms may take example by it and
acknowledge that from God alone proceed success
or the misfortunes of men. And seeing we ought to
have recourse to him alone, let us beseech him to assist
and advise us in all our afflictions for in this world there
is nothing else, of which the great ones have their share
as well as the meanest of us all. Wherein he manifesteth
his own greatness, in that neither King nor prince are
exempted from his correcting hand, and who stand not
continually in need of him and his divine assistance.[1]

Francis was in the Loire Valley when he celebrated his
fortieth birthday in September 1534, nearing the twen-
tieth year of his reign. At such a landmark point in any
human life, there is perhaps a natural tendency to look back as
much as forwards. If Francis felt such an impulse, he might have
been reasonably pleased at where he found himself that autumn.
He had experienced what the French military captain Blaise de
Lasseran-Massencôme, seigneur de Monluc (1500/1501−1577),
reflected in his *Commentaires* was the lot of kings and commoners
alike. Francis's health was generally good, if still affected by out-
breaks of fever and other symptoms of disease. He was happy
in his relationship with Anne d'Heilly. His three sons and two

surviving daughters were growing to early adulthood, and the
succession seemed secure. His personal authority had very largely
recovered from the crisis of 1525–6 and he was once more a king
of France to be reckoned with. His realm was at peace and continuing to develop economically, increasing its trade and its commercial infrastructure. He was engaged in a building programme
that gave him great personal satisfaction and demonstrated the
wealth of the crown and its sophistication. His personal style as
king had once more rekindled the enthusiasm of the French
nobility and secured the cooperation of the majority of provincial institutions and elites throughout the country. Time, perhaps,
for him to concentrate on nurturing what he already had, as ruler
of Europe's most powerful unitary royal state? That was certainly the view of his rivals. Yet one problem still clouded Francis's
otherwise sunny horizons: Milan.

The Treaty of Cambrai of 1529 is arguably the most effective
agreement that Francis ever made with Charles v. This is because
it resulted in the longest period of peace between them. During
its continuance, Francis recovered and consolidated his authority
in France without external threats. It did not, however, fundamentally alter the king's outlook on his place in the world. Even
during the treaty's currency, he did all he could to weaken Charles
and build his own strength against him through alliances. As we
have seen, from 1526 Francis fought determinedly to safeguard
his kingdom from within against religious unorthodoxy of all
kinds. In this effort, and in his international relations more generally, reconciliation and cooperation with the papacy became
part of his strategy to isolate Charles. Since repudiating the French
in 1529 after the failed siege of Naples, Clement VII had grown
weary (and wary) of Charles's power in Italy. He had met Charles
and crowned him emperor at Bologna in 1530, but their relations
had rapidly cooled thereafter. Conversely, relations with Francis
slowly improved, focusing now on negotiations for a marriage

between Catherine de' Medici (conventionally called the pope's niece, but in fact a distant cousin) and Francis's son Henri, duc d'Orléans. A marriage into the French royal line would be a tremendous coup for Clement's Florentine dynasty, and the pope also sought to give himself room for manoeuvre against Charles. Francis was given permission to levy another *décime*, and there is some evidence of his promising to cede the cities of Parma and Piacenza to Clement, should he ever be in a position to do so.

Even as he did all he could to win over the pope and to suppress heresy at home, Francis offered support to the members of the Schmalkaldic League. The league was formed by a group of German Protestant princes in February 1531, partly in response to the election of Ferdinand of Austria, the emperor's brother, as king of the Romans. This, the 'Protestant' princes said, was an act without constitutional precedent. Presenting himself as the defender of true German liberties, Francis agreed to the Treaty of Scheyern with the league in May 1532.

This committed him to paying 100,000 *écus* towards a planned war against Charles. To meet this obligation, Francis needed financial assistance and was therefore also careful to maintain good relations, as far as he could, with Henry of England, his 'good brother, friend and perpetual ally', as they now habitually addressed each other. Although Wolsey had died in disgrace in 1530, the Boleyn family, who had done more than anyone else to oust the cardinal, had thereafter maintained his pacific policy towards France. Francis had assisted Henry during 1530 by allowing him to consult several French universities on the validity or otherwise of his marriage, then putting pressure on their faculties of theology to find for the English king. Eager, himself, to secure further support, Henry had expressed interest to Francis in February 1532 in 'some new and more special conjunction than hath yet been between us', and had already offered some money towards Francis's German plans. Francis at first responded coolly to the offer, but with the Scheyern treaty concluded, he showed greater interest in Henry's money. Thus, in June, a new alliance was agreed whereby Francis would come to Henry's military assistance if ever he were attacked by the emperor and as he pursued his quarrel with the papacy. True, the force to be provided under the terms of the treaty was little more than a token one, but it was the first and only time a king of France ever committed himself to the defence of England. The alliance treaty was sworn to in London in September 1532. At the same ceremony, Henry created Anne Boleyn (c. 1500–1536) Marquess of Pembroke in her own right, making her the highest-ranking noblewoman in his kingdom after Queen Katherine and Princess Mary.

The following month, the two kings met for the second and final time in their lives, to celebrate their renewed alliance and, ostensibly, to plan joint action against the Ottomans. The meeting was a scaled-down version of the Field of Cloth of Gold. There was no jousting this time, but plenty of feasting and dancing. Francis hosted Henry at Boulogne-sur-Mer for several days from 21 October. He presented his three sons to Henry and they gave him very studied public thanks for his help in securing the release of the two eldest boys from Spain two years earlier. Henry then entertained Francis and his court at Calais. Anne was with him, in the expectation that Francis would receive her formally, effectively endorsing her relationship with Henry. This Francis would not do, but he and Anne did evidently have a private conversation at one point. Expensive presents were again exchanged, including a very ornate camp bed for Henry. After the meeting, Henry Howard, Earl of Surrey (1517–1547), and Henry's natural son Henry Fitzroy, Duke of Richmond (1519–1536), remained in France for some months as guests of the dauphin and his brothers.

This meeting has often been dismissed by historians as even less significant than the Field of Cloth of Gold because it apparently had few consequences for Anglo-French dealings, and it is true that the terms of that year's treaty were never acted upon. Yet it was still significant for Francis's reign because very soon afterwards Henry and Anne were secretly married. They finally consummated their relationship and Anne became pregnant. For that to have happened, Anne had evidently to be convinced – and after ten years of courtship, all the while refusing Henry a full sexual relationship – that things would now be well. At the Calais meeting, Henry later said, Francis had promised that he would not allow a Valois–Medici marriage alliance unless and until Clement resolved Henry's matrimonial dilemma. Francis denied ever having given so specific an undertaking, saying that it was only when the Orléans marriage had taken place that he would be able, as the pope's kinsman, to do anything useful for Henry.

Whatever was really said and whatever Henry thought, Anne's pregnancy was confirmed by March and revealed to Francis by her brother George, who was sent as ambassador that spring. Despite Francis's desperate exhortations to keep the matter secret, the pregnancy forced Henry to act decisively within England. His first marriage was pronounced invalid by Convocation and Archbishop Thomas Cranmer (1489–1556), and that to Anne was confirmed in English law. She was crowned queen on 1 June 1533. Jean de Dinteville, then the resident French ambassador, took – somewhat reluctantly, it seems – a prominent part in the queen's coronation procession through London, where at least some of the crowd shouted abuse at him, as a Frenchman. Around this time he also commissioned from Hans Holbein what has become one of the icons of High Renaissance art, the double portrait of himself and his friend Georges de Selve (1508–1541) known as *The Ambassadors*. It is a fine study of the two men, painted when Selve was in England on a mission to do with Henry's marriage. Its arcane symbolism alludes cryptically, but quite directly, to the distressed state of contemporary Christendom, and to France's potentially powerful role in resolving the growing struggle between orthodoxy and dissent.[2]

Henry looked to Francis to fulfil his promise of help in preventing any rupture between himself and the papacy. This Francis sincerely wanted to provide, even if he also saw the advantages to himself of Henry's greater dependence on him, as the king of England busily alienated himself from both pope and emperor. In October Francis met Clement at Marseilles and apparently urged patience with Henry upon the Holy Father. There, on the 28th of the month, Henri d'Orléans married Catherine de' Medici (1519–1589) without any resolution of Henry's dilemma. Henry was appalled when he heard the news. But by that stage, with the English king's second marriage an accomplished fact, Francis could have done little for Henry. Moreover, what good he did do, he later told Henry, was undone by English ambassadors sent to the pope while he was at Marseilles; they had threatened Clement with a General Council of the Church if the threat of papal sanction on Henry were not lifted. Five months later the pope duly excommunicated Henry, who immediately renounced obedience to Rome and went on to establish his royal supremacy over the Church in England in 1534. Henry's actions sometimes embarrassed Francis, but an isolated England also suited him well enough. He had hoped to build on his improved relationship with Clement to press his claim to Milan and have papal support for another effort to wrest it from Charles by force if necessary. Yet, less than a year after their meeting, the pope died, rendering the Orléans marriage little more than a *mésalliance*. In October Alessandro Farnese (1468–1549), a member of the resolutely pro-imperial family who dominated the area to the north of the papal states, became Pope Paul III.

Even as he had built relations with the papacy and with German Protestant princes, and tried to turn Henry's matrimonial dilemma to his own advantage, Francis had also begun exploring the possibility of an alliance with the Ottoman sultan, Süleyman. After the death of Louis II of Hungary at the Battle of Mohács in 1526, Francis had been drawn to support John Zápolyai, the Vayvode of Transylvania, who, with Ottoman support, disputed the succession to the kingdom of Hungary with Ferdinand of Habsburg. It proved difficult for Zápolyai to make good his claim against such powerful competition, and in the autumn of 1528 Francis offered him assistance in return for the Vayvode agreeing to name Henri d'Orléans as his successor should he die without an heir. This, in turn, drew Francis further into the Ottoman orbit. He hoped Ottoman military power might be used to his advantage, without threatening the alliance with the German Protestant princes. He could not afford to be seen by them to be encouraging the Ottomans to attack German lands, even if they were Habsburg territory.

The Ottomans attacked Vienna in the summer of 1529 but retreated again in October that year as their fighting season ended. Süleyman thereafter increased his presence in the Mediterranean even as he turned his armies towards Persia. In 1534 a fleet of 160 ships under his admiral Hayre-ad-dîn (1466/83–1546), also known as 'Barbarossa', entered the Mediterranean. He had spent the last half-a-dozen years as military agent and vassal of the sultan, launching raids from Algiers against the Balearic Islands, Sicily and the southern shores of the Italian mainland. Now he seized Tunis from the local, unpopular Arab overlord and Spanish vassal, Muley Hassan. From there, Hayre-ad-dîn's fleets could harass Spanish shipping and coastal territories. Charles appreciated the seriousness of the threat and began making preparations for responsive action. His councillors advised caution, warning that Francis might take the opportunity to invade Italy once more. Charles, however, secured the support of Paul III against that eventuality and, with mounting excitement, determined to force Hayre-ad-dîn out of Tunis. He sailed with a large fleet on 30 May 1535 and, in the course of the following two months, destroyed most of Hayre-ad-dîn's fleet and achieved the first significant personal military victory of his life. He led his troops in taking the fortified port of La Goletta and the city of Tunis itself, which he entered in triumph on 21 July. Hayre-ad-dîn retreated to Algiers with the remnant of his fleet.

Having pacified Tunis, Charles then sailed to Sicily and from there made victorious entries into towns as he advanced through southern Italy, known as the kingdom of Naples, the claim to which he had inherited from Ferdinand of Aragon. He arrived in Rome at Easter 1536, and was greeted as a Christian hero who had saved the south of the peninsula from the Ottoman scourge. It was in effect the high point of his reign, when, for the only time, it seemed that all of Christendom was behind him and what he had achieved, and that he was – briefly at least – in fact as well as name, the Holy Roman Emperor.

Charles's hold on Italy in general had never seemed stronger, and in one view this was enhanced by the death in November 1535 of Francesco Sforza, who had been, in effect, incumbent duke of Milan since Pavia in 1525. His young widow was Charles's niece Christina of Denmark. She would soon be touted as a possible fourth wife for Henry of England, and painted by Holbein in that cause. In the absence of Sforza heirs, the duchy escheated to the emperor directly and, in Charles's view at least, extinguished the Orléans claim to it through the pre-existing Visconti line. Francis watched the triumph of his great rival, grim-faced. He insisted that his son Henri, as the current duc d'Orléans, was entitled to the duchy and that it should be made over to him. Through Catherine, Henri also had a claim to the duchy of Urbino, and that made him unacceptable to Charles as duke of Milan.

Claiming to be acting in defence of his legitimate rights, and presumably intending to strengthen his position relative to Milan, in February 1536 Francis took the extraordinary decision to invade the duchy of Savoy. It was ruled by Charles III, duc de Savoie (1486–1553), who was not only Francis's uncle (as the half-brother of his mother), but the brother-in-law of the emperor through his marriage to Beatrice of Portugal (1504–1538), the sister of Charles V's wife, Isabella. By the end of March the French army, led by Admiral Philippe Chabot, had captured most of Savoy's territory and moved on to Turin, the capital of Piedmont. The swift campaign was militarily successful but, given the threat it posed to Milan and Lombardy, also highly provocative strategically. Charles V responded by demanding that all troops be withdrawn from Piedmont while offering Francis the duchy of Milan for his youngest son, Charles d'Angoulême, not Henri d'Orléans. That, or Charles would meet Francis in single combat to determine the future of Burgundy and Milan in a decisive encounter. Privately, he knew that neither prospect would be genuinely acceptable to Francis. Francis duly responded that he was merely pursuing ancestral rights and had not infringed the Treaty of Cambrai, and that his armies had not set foot on imperial territory. Charles therefore had nothing to complain about. Francis accepted the emperor's personal challenge, also probably confident that Charles's advisors would never let it come to anything.

Pope Paul offered to mediate but, still full of confidence after his victory in Tunis, Charles preferred to fight. Claiming to be acting in defence of his relative Charles de Savoie, the emperor launched an invasion of Provence in July 1536. His frustration with Francis was plain, and he doubtless wanted to push the French back within their own borders, destroy their capacity to threaten Milan again, and perhaps even gain some territory with which to bargain with Francis. In something of a reprise of Bourbon's campaign of 1524, the emperor's army made rapid initial progress westwards, reaching the area around Aix-en-Provence by 5 August. In response, Francis ordered Chabot to hold his position in Piedmont and, as in 1524, a royal army was brought south. Francis himself remained at Valence, while Anne de Montmorency took tactical charge of the campaign from his headquarters at a fortified camp at Avignon. Montmorency deployed a form of 'scorched-earth' policy, evacuating Aix and ordering the destruction of all means of sustenance for the advancing imperial army. He fortified Marseilles and stationed a fleet of galleys offshore there, while also reinforcing towns along the Rhône. Charles took Aix but could get no further west or north than had Bourbon twelve years earlier.

The emperor held out for a month before the outbreak of disease among his troops forced him to retreat towards Italy. Some effort was made to avoid a repeat of Bourbon's headlong flight back along the coast. Nevertheless, in his wake Charles left, according to one source, 'men and horses all piled in heaps, the dying mixed up with the dead. Whoever saw the desolation could not consider it less than what Josephus described during the destruction of Jerusalem.'[3] From Genoa, Charles embarked for Spain in late September. Embarrassed by his failure, he was, as Michelangelo noted, mocked in Rome for his strategic ineptitude as a 'crab who moved backwards when he wanted to go forwards'.

Benvenuto Cellini, *Medal for Francis I*, 1537, lead.

Roman satirists even gave a new twist to his 'Plus Ultra' motto, which they altered to 'Non Plus Ultra Rhodanus' (No Further than the Rhône).[4] Whether it was owing to his own instincts or, as Bellay surmised, Montmorency's staying hand, Francis showed greater strategic acumen than Charles. Not only had he prevented the emperor from getting beyond the Rhône, but moreover, in resisting a headlong pursuit as Charles retreated, Francis had saved himself effort and treasure. The king had evidently learned from the debacle of 1525 something about the risks of impetuosity in warfare.

Notwithstanding this moment of triumph, Francis suffered a great personal loss at that time. On 10 August the dauphin François died suddenly at Tournus after drinking a glass of iced water following a game of tennis. None but the king's close friend Jean, Cardinal of Lorraine, dared to confirm the news to him. The cause of death was probably natural, but poison was immediately suspected and one Sebastiano de Montecuculli, a servant of the young prince who had served him the water, apparently confessed under torture and was publicly executed at Lyon with all the cruelty at the command of the sixteenth-century state. Francis accused Charles of complicity in murder, an imperial safe conduct having been found in the servant's possession. The emperor vigorously denied the accusation and fought on. While Charles battled in Provence, another imperial army under Henry of Nassau had attacked across northern France towards the Somme. Francis responded by declaring forfeit the counties of Flanders, Artois and Charolais, which the emperor held as fiefs of the French crown. He moved immediately to counter-attack and took the best advantage he could of Charles's defeat in the south. The campaign resumed in the spring of 1537 and Francis took back a number of towns in Artois.

In the autumn of 1536 James V of Scotland (1512–1542) joined the French court at Lyon, then still in mourning for the dauphin.

Since his childhood, James had looked to France for support in maintaining the independence of Scotland from Henry VIII's determination to be its overlord, and he had come to see Francis as a mentor, even a father figure. For his part, Francis usually addressed James as 'very dear and most loved brother and son'. In November James was part of a hunting party in which the new dauphin, Henri, was saved partly by luck and partly by his own skill and strength when a huge boar charged directly at him. On New Year's Day 1537 James married Francis's daughter Madeleine at Notre-Dame in Paris, at which ceremony Catherine de' Medici made her public debut as the new dauphine. Festive banquets and jousts followed at the Louvre. Tragically, Madeleine died, aged just seventeen, on 7 July, barely six weeks after she had arrived at Leith. James was soon back in France, and in May 1538 he and Marie de Guise (1515–1560), the eldest child of Claude de Lorraine, were married by proxy. She had previously been married, briefly, to Louis II d'Orléans, duc de Longueville (1510–1537), and had attended James's wedding to Madeleine in 1537. Marie's formal marriage ceremony took place at St Andrews on 17 June 1538, amid great celebrations, including a tournament and banquets.

By then, fighting between Francis and Charles had petered out. Financially exhausted, the two men were forced into a grudging truce. Although peace negotiations began under Charles's sister Mary, his regent in the Netherlands, they collapsed almost immediately. The emperor then proposed Paul III as an intermediary, and so great was the present distrust between himself and Francis that it seemed no less a figure could resolve their differences. After some initial resistance from Francis, talks began that led to bilateral meetings between the king, the pope and the emperor in Nice between 15 May and 20 June 1538. Francis rejected Paul's suggestion that Ferdinand of Habsburg's daughter should marry Charles d'Angoulême and that the duchy of Milan be made over to them after three years. Strongly encouraged by Montmorency, however, he did agree to meet Charles in July at Aigues-Mortes in Languedoc, at the eastern edge of the Rhône delta, the river that had been the barrier between them two years earlier.

Charles sailed into the port on 14 July 1538. Francis was already there and, instead of waiting to meet the emperor on land as agreed, the king had himself rowed out on a small boat to greet Charles on board his galley as soon as it had dropped anchor. This unexpected gesture was interpreted as a great compliment to Charles, even as it was also disconcerting. It was prompted by Francis's desire not only to express evident trust in his enemy, but to seize the initiative in their encounter. It forced Charles to receive Francis in a reciprocal manner, and the emperor actually reached his arm down to help Francis up a ladder to board the vessel. Francis did not leave things there. Charles landed the following day and, after dining at midday, retired for a siesta in his lodgings. On being told some hours later that the emperor had awoken, Francis arrived unannounced and burst into Charles's room, greeting him effusively. The emperor was still in bed and not fully dressed. Instantly, he got to his feet to greet the king of France, who was dressed splendidly. Francis gave him a diamond ring worth 30,000 crowns as a gift, betokening good faith.[5] This visit directly recalled Francis's impromptu visit to Henry in his castle at the Field of Cloth of Gold in 1520 and, as on that occasion, his unwilling host had to 'counter-attack' as best he could. Charles placed a collar of the Order of the Golden Fleece, perhaps hurriedly snatched from one of his close gentlemen, around the French king's neck. In response, Francis triumphantly removed his own collar of the Order of Saint-Michel and placed it about Charles's shoulders. Although they had been members of each other's chivalric orders since youth, the exchange implied a renewed acknowledgement of the honour code between the two men as knights, and was seen by most as a diplomatic triumph for Francis.

The result of the meeting at Aigues-Mortes was an informal 'entente' between the two rulers. Francis would keep peace with Charles and, at a time to be determined, Charles would convey sovereignty over Milan to Francis's youngest son, who would be married into the Habsburg orbit. Wider reactions to this personal meeting were favourable and it proved enough to give some impetus to further efforts at reconciliation. Francis met Mary of Hungary at Compiègne in October 1538 and concluded an agreement that went some way to settling the perennial disputes along the border between France and the Netherlands.[6]

The entente reached at Aigues-Mortes was enough to worry Henry in England and the German Protestants, all of whom feared being abandoned by Francis in their ongoing disputes with Charles. Afraid of some joint action against him, Henry demanded that Francis honour the terms of the agreements between them and began fortifying the south coast of his kingdom with newly designed angled-bastioned forts, which can still be seen today at Walmer, Deal, Falmouth and elsewhere. Henry also entered negotiations that culminated in late 1539 in an alliance with William, Duke of Julich-Cleves-Berg (1516–1592), sealed by the king's marriage (his fourth) to the duke's sister, Anne (1515–1557). She was also the sister-in-law of John Frederick I, Elector of Saxony (1503–1554), the leader of the Schmalkaldic League.

Charles was sufficiently reassured at Aigues-Mortes that, when he returned to Spain, he decided to follow up his victory at Tunis with an attack on Algiers, which was still under Ottoman overlordship. His Spanish subjects were rather less enthusiastic, given the cost of his recent Provençal debacle, and the nobles of the Cortes of Castile told him flatly that he could forget a proposed excise tax to help fund this adventure. Of course, Castile was not so subject to the predations of the corsairs as were other parts of the Iberian kingdoms.

The empress Isabella was again pregnant by the end of the year. In May 1539 she was delivered of a stillborn child and, tragically, she died soon afterwards. Charles went into a long period of grief. From this he was wrenched only by another refusal of taxation, in his native city of Ghent, Flanders. In August 1539 its leaders refused to pay his demands and expressed discontent at his continued absence from his northern realms, and within weeks, his sister told him, the city was in open revolt. Habsburg authority throughout the Netherlands was challenged as it had not been for generations. With winter coming on, Charles ruled out sailing to Flanders from Santander and instead tried a new approach to Francis. Through his ambassador, he asked his 'good cousin' if he might pass through France to Ghent. He also asked Francis to help him deceive his own allies and his Spanish subjects as to the origins of the invitation, requesting that Francis write 'affectionate letters to persuade me to make this journey'. He indicated that he would reciprocate with action about Milan, but that this should not be discussed between them during his time in France.

Francis's initial reaction to these extraordinary requests was negative, as might be imagined. He was within his rights to refuse such a suggestion. Charles's request was presumptuous, yet it was of a piece with the expressions of trust that the two men had exchanged the previous summer. Montmorency encouraged him, and the king finally agreed. He issued a fulsome invitation, seconded by leading members of the French court, 'signed and written of my own hand' to Charles as his 'best brother and cousin'.[7]

The French were determined to be conspicuously generous and honourable hosts, in the hope that the emperor would respond in a similar vein over the question of Milan. But by the time Charles's visit began with his arrival at Bayonne on 27 November 1539, Francis was ill, and he travelled as far south as Loches in a litter. He ensured that Charles was received with processions, triumphal arches and gifts in all the principal towns of his route, and he escorted the emperor to the royal châteaux of the Loire and on to Fontainebleau, where he spent Christmas. Francis, whose health had recovered somewhat by then, gave banquets in his guests' honour and certainly showed Charles the newly completed Galerie François 1er. On New Year's Day Charles was received in Paris with welcoming crowds and more triumphal arches and orations. All this was designed to impress and even intimidate Charles with the apparent wealth of France, its wish for peace and its contented unity under its apparently much-loved sovereign – in pointed contrast to Charles's rebellious Flemish subjects, of course. In the early days of January, Francis accompanied the emperor to the border, during which time Charles apparently gave informal indications that, in light of the honours paid to him, once he reached Brussels he and Francis could 'do what needs to be done' in respect of Milan.

This was the high point in relations between Francis and Charles during their whole lives. More than any other, it was Anne de Montmorency, the man who proved to be the most successful minister and courtier of the French Renaissance, who was responsible. Since becoming the king's right-hand man in 1526, he had advocated a reconciliation between Francis and Charles. While working hard to secure the king's release from Spain, he had also worked with Cardinal Wolsey in 1527 for the 'Eternal Peace' agreed that year, when he had led an embassy to present Henry with the insignia of the Order of Saint-Michel. He had helped to fashion and implement the Treaty of Cambrai in 1529, and since advised Francis to maintain the peace. He closely oversaw arrangements for the release of the two French princes from Spain in 1530. From the mid-1520s onwards, Montmorency had also steadily built an extensive network of clients and adherents across the noble and urban elites of the kingdom. When the king was at peace, the royal household was at its largest and, being its chief supervising officer, he enjoyed the strongest influence and patronage, so he saw peace as being good in principle as well as to the king's advantage, and his own.[8]

Montmorency's advocacy of peace led to rivalry with Admiral Chabot, who tended to back a more aggressive policy towards Charles. Chabot's influence eclipsed Montmorency's briefly in 1536, when Francis decided, against Montmorency's advice, to invade Savoy. He was soon enough recalled to power, however, when Charles counter-attacked. As we have seen, contemporaries credited Montmorency for the French defensive strategy that brought the imperial invasion to a halt. In 1538 he was rewarded with the office of Constable of France, becoming the kingdom's chief military commander after the king, the position formerly held by Charles, duc de Bourbon. This enhanced Montmorency's personal authority still further, adding to that he had enjoyed over the royal household as *Grand Maître* since 1526 and giving him extensive patronage in recruiting officers and men to the army, their commands and deployment. Even from this powerful position, Montmorency still advocated peace with Charles in 1539 more fervently than ever before. He had very largely overseen the arrangements for the emperor's visit that year during Francis's illness and, with the dauphin Henri and the duc d'Orléans, had ensured that Charles was shown every honour and expression of trust during his time in France.

Charles's journey through Francis's kingdom was met with disbelief throughout Europe. What followed brought a similar reaction from Francis and his close courtiers. For, once he had settled the rebellion in Ghent, in March 1540 Charles overturned the understood basis for the continuing friendship with Francis. Rather than arranging for the time and place for Charles d'Orléans to be invested with Milan, as Francis understood would be the basis of a permanent peace, he said that the king's eldest son should instead marry his daughter Maria of Austria (1528–1603). That done, he would become joint lieutenant and co-heir with her to

the Netherlands, Charolais and Burgundy. He should also be endowed with extensive lands within France. If Maria had no heirs at her death, the provinces would revert to the Habsburgs. He also proposed that his son Philip (1527–1598) should marry Francis's niece Jeanne d'Albret (1528–1572), heiress to Navarre. In return for this magnanimity, as he saw it, Francis should renounce all claims on Milan and Savoy and, if he did so, Charles would renounce Burgundy once and for all.

Geoffrey Parker, the emperor's most recent academic biographer, describes Charles as 'oblivious' to the total unacceptability of these proposals to the French. Apparently, he could not see how his solution to the long-standing problem of the porous frontier between France and imperial territories to its north, south and east was not welcome. He clearly intended to incorporate the kingdom of Navarre into Spain by the marriage, something the French crown had ever striven to prevent. He appeared

Taddeo Zuccaro, *Francis I Receiving Emperor Charles V and Cardinal Alessandro Farnese in Paris in 1540, c.* 1557–66, fresco, Palazzo Farnese, Caprarola.

not to notice that the creation of a virtual appanage within France for Orléans resembled the situation of Burgundy a century earlier, or the position of Bourbon before his rebellion, and therefore created a problem for Francis as king. Above all, he apparently *still* did not comprehend how sincerely Francis held his claim to Milan, which had driven Francis's whole foreign policy from the day of his accession in 1515. The prospect of future sovereignty for Francis's youngest son over the Netherlands instead of Milan had no appeal for Francis whatsoever.[9]

Perhaps Charles did realize all these things, and disregarded them in order to create problems for his enemy. The announcement certainly humiliated Francis, so soon after he had shown Charles generous hospitality in France, during a visit the emperor himself had requested. Charles went further, turning insult into active injury. In October 1540, without even notifying Francis in advance, he invested his son Philip with the duchy of Milan as an imperial fief. This was done, he said, for the duchy's own protection, 'should it fall into hostile hands or those of someone unable to defend it' – a less than oblique and sarcastic reference to Francis.[10] Francis never trusted Charles again. Moreover, his precipitate action undermined the very man who had always supported Valois–Habsburg peace, Anne de Montmorency. As the English ambassador to France Sir John Wallop (*c.* 1490–1551) reported, from the time of the announcement of Charles's proposals in March 1540, Montmorency lost his grip on power. He was no longer called to the council, nor written to by ambassadors and advisors in the way they had once routinely done, as to the king.

In light of these developments, Francis resumed his policy of securing allies against Charles wherever he could. His main focus now was not England, as it once would have been, but rather the far more powerful Ottomans. Francis restored relations with Süleyman that had been strained during the apparent reconciliation with Charles. Antonio Rincon (d. 1541), a Spanish-born diplomat in French service, was sent to explain Francis's disappointed hopes over Milan and to encourage the sultan's action against the Habsburgs. In July 1541 Rincon and a colleague were murdered by imperial troops while travelling down the Po to Venice on a second mission to Constantinople. Francis held Charles responsible for the killing.

Francis was also approached by William of Cleves, who had been recognized as duke of Guelders despite Charles's opposition. He sought protection from both England and France against the emperor but the marriage in January 1540 of his sister Anne to Henry was disastrous and was annulled within months. In its wake, Henry lost interest in Cleves, but was also somewhat more committed to renewing his alliance with Francis. On hearing that Henry had been ill at the start of 1541, Francis sent his 'good brother and perpetual ally' some pasties made from deer and boar that he had hunted. The French ambassador to England at the time, Charles de Marillac (c. 1510–1560), hunted with Henry as he accompanied him north to York in the summer of that year to meet James V (who never turned up). Marillac pursued nego-tiations for a renewed alliance with England centred on a marriage between Charles d'Orléans and Princess Mary. Marillac's imperial counterpart, Eustace Chapuys (c. 1490–1556), also sought an alliance with Henry. As Marillac appreciated, there were numerous outstanding disputes over existing agreements between Henry and Francis that hampered his own negotiations, chiefly the fact of Francis's not having paid the annual pensions due to Henry under the terms of their various alliances.[11]

By the summer of 1541 an alliance had been agreed between Francis and Cleves, secured by the hand in marriage of the king's twelve-year-old niece Jeanne d'Albret. Such a close alliance with a Protestant prince was repugnant to Montmorency. Marguerite, her mother, also objected on the grounds of Jeanne's age. After

being ordered on his allegiance to carry the girl to the altar for
her wedding, Montmorency withdrew to his estates and from
political life. Yet, by contrast with the fall of several other great
royal ministers of the period, he was never formally deprived
of all his offices; he merely ceased to exercise them. The offices
of *Grand Maître* and Constable went into obeyance for the rest of
Francis's reign, and the only office that was taken from Montmorency was the governorship of Languedoc. This was done in
such a way as to spare Montmorency's pride as far as possible, a
fact that speaks of Francis's continuing regard for his servant
and childhood friend, and of his own style as king. In May 1542
the king rescinded the powers of all provincial governors on
technical grounds. Two days later all the governors were reinstated
except one, Montmorency. He never saw Francis again.[12]

With Montmorency's withdrawal from public life, a new and
slightly larger group of advisors and ministers emerged, among
whose principal members was Montmorency's rival Chabot. As
Admiral in succession to Bonnivet and governor of Burgundy
from 1526 he had been involved in the king's government. He
had distinguished himself defending Marseilles against Bourbon
in 1524 and led the conquest of Turin in 1536. He had also played
his part in welcoming the emperor in 1539 but, probably owing
to Montmorency, had not had a very central role in the peace
negotiations at Aigues-Mortes that had led to the brief entente.
Chabot, too, was soon in trouble, however. In 1540 Chancellor
Guillaume Poyet (*c.* 1473–1548), who had made his name in the
service of the crown against Bourbon, held an enquiry that found
Chabot guilty of financial malpractice as Admiral and as governor of Burgundy. He was deprived of all his offices and im-
prisoned at Vincennes. After Montmorency's fall, Chabot's
convictions were quashed and he was restored to all his offices,
most likely with the assistance (if not at the insistence) of both
Madame d'Étampes and Marguerite de Navarre, and possibly

also Charles d'Orléans, to whom the two noblewomen gravitated as a counterpoint to the dauphin Henri, his wife, Catherine de' Medici, and his mistress Diane de Poitiers. The overturning of Chabot's conviction brought the focus on the chancellor who had overseen it. He was himself arrested for an apparently unrelated lapse in his own duties. What the ultimate implications of all this might have been for the Admiral and court can only be imagined as, in October, Chabot suffered a sudden collapse. He died in June 1543.

With Chabot's death, Francis lost the last member of the generation of advisors who had grown up with him. Two younger men, until then in the second rank of councillors, now increasingly ran the king's affairs. The first was Claude d'Annebault (1495–1552), who was made Admiral in February 1544. He succeeded to Chabot's duties as a military officer, but did not hold his predecessor's view that Francis should always maintain an aggressive stance towards Charles, even as he also shared Madame d'Étampes' view that supporting the German Protestants was key to the king's interests. The extent of his actual influence on the king over that of d'Étampes is debatable, and he has been accused of trimming his sails to the prevailing royal winds. His advice was at best nuanced, and at worst confused.[13] This was countered to some extent by Francis's other principal advisor in the early 1540s, François de Tournon (1489–1562). Archbishop successively of Embrun and of Bourges, in 1525 he had joined Louise de Savoie's regency council and by 1529 he was working with Montmorency, supervising the collection of the ransom needed to secure the release of the two princes in Spain. He was made a cardinal in March 1530 and was part of the French entourage that escorted the two princes back to France that July. Appointed ambassador to Rome in 1532, he urged sympathy for Henry VIII's plight on Clement, but never to the detriment of his own sovereign's interests with the Holy See. In 1540 he was

made chancellor of the Order of Saint-Michel. With Montmorency's fall, he undertook much of the day-to-day running of
the royal administration, particularly its financial aspects, drawing
on the experience he had gained since the 1520s, and he remained
the king's close confidant until the end of Francis's reign. After
the accession of Henri II he was excluded from power, but he
was made archbishop of Lyon in 1551. Strictly orthodox throughout his life, Tournon participated in the Colloquy of Poissy in
1561 and that at Saint-Germain-en-Laye, where he died in April
1562.[14]

Another churchman whom Francis took into his confidence
in these years was Jean du Bellay (1492/8–1560). He had been
ambassador to England periodically between 1529 and 1531, occasionally joined by his brother Guillaume (1491–1543). As much
a client of Montmorency as of the king, Jean du Bellay amassed
seven bishoprics or archbishoprics, including Bayonne and Paris
(the latter in 1532), and twenty abbacies under royal patronage.
He was made a cardinal in 1535 but became important in papal
politics in Rome itself only after Francis's death. He was more
sympathetic to calls for reform than was Tournon, and several
times had to defend himself from accusations of heresy. He became
the king's lieutenant-general in Paris and the Île-de-France,
advised Francis as a member of his council, and was one of those
responsible for the defence of the capital during the imperial
and English incursions of 1537 and 1542–4.[15]

The 1540s also brought the rise to prominence of the Guise
family. Claude de Lorraine, who was two years the king's junior,
had been raised with Francis as a child and was an important army
commander throughout the 1520s. The dukedom of Lorraine was
outside the sovereignty of France, and in 1528 the king created
Claude duc de Guise and *prince étranger* (foreign peer) of France.
Claude worked closely with Jean du Bellay on the defence of
northern France in 1536–7, and his younger brother Jean was also

close to the king. To advance his family's standing, Jean was made
cardinal of Lorraine in 1518, but he had no vocation and was
known more for his artistic patronage and love affairs than for
any churchmanship. He was a member of the king's conciliar
circle from 1530 and represented Francis in talks with Charles
over Milan on several occasions in 1540–41. He also assisted the
king with extravagant hospitality given to ambassadors and
high-ranking visitors to the court.

In the early autumn of 1541 the emperor renewed his war
against the Ottomans in the Mediterranean. Hayre-ad-dîn had
recovered from the loss of Tunis in 1536 and had since attacked
the southern coasts of Spain and Sicily, and the Italian mainland,
taking thousands into slavery. In 1541, however, he was supporting Süleyman's next attack on Hungary. Buda fell to the sultan
in August. While there was little to be done about that, Charles
decided that it was now an opportune moment to attack Hayre-
ad-dîn's base at Algiers. This time he had better political and
financial support from his Iberian kingdoms. He reached his
objective in October, but barely had his main force landed than
a reinforcement fleet was scattered in a storm off the African
coast. Without these supplies, Charles had to withdraw, leaving thousands of men behind. They were overwhelmed by the
Algerian counter-attack and became prisoners of war and
Ottoman galley slaves. Renewed Franco-Ottoman talks followed and Francis secured from Süleyman his promise of greater
support, both in Hungary and in the western Mediterranean.
A French port was to be made available to harbour a fleet of
150 vessels.

Having secured that promise, in July 1542 Francis declared
war on Charles again. The murder of Rincon was the ostensible
cause, but Francis included a long list of complaints against
the emperor's actions, 'repugnant to all divine and human law',
which he could no longer brook. An army nominally under the

command of Charles d'Orléans took Luxembourg, and another
led by the dauphin Henri and Annebault attacked Perpignan at
the foot of the Pyrenees. Rather as in 1521, however, the French
were finally repelled on both fronts and Francis had also to deal
with a revolt in Brittany over the salt tax or *gabelle*. This required
his personal intervention before it was resolved at the end of the
year, but a compromise was reached whereby Francis pardoned
the rebel salt towns and they paid him an indemnity in salt, which
he could use to pay some of his debts.

Charles V took no immediate retaliatory action to the assaults
of 1542 beyond repelling them and securing his borders. Something of a 'phoney war' ensued while he sought finally to conclude
an alliance with England. Henry, for his part, was infuriated by
James V's indifference to him at York. He turned against Scotland
more forcefully than he had done in thirty years, and the autumn
campaign in 1542 ended in the defeat of more than 15,000 Scots
at the Battle of Solway Moss, in the aftermath of which James,
one-time son-in-law and protégé of Francis, died. His infant
daughter Mary Stuart (1542–1587) inherited the crown and James
Hamilton, Earl of Arran (*c.* 1517–1575), became regent. The Scots
rapidly renewed their ancient alliance with France while, just as
Marillac had feared, Henry concluded a secret alliance with
Charles in February 1543. Its core provision was for a joint invasion of France to be undertaken within two years. War was formally declared less than six months later, in June, after Francis
was presented with an ultimatum that he had no hope of meeting.
The English began raiding the Boulonnais from their base in
Calais, but the action was largely at sea for the remainder of
that year.

By then, Francis was also fighting in Brabant, where Charles
moved against William of Cleves, wanting to seize the duchy of
Guelders from him. An imperial army was moved down the Rhine
from Speyer to Bonn and attacked Düren. Francis again attacked

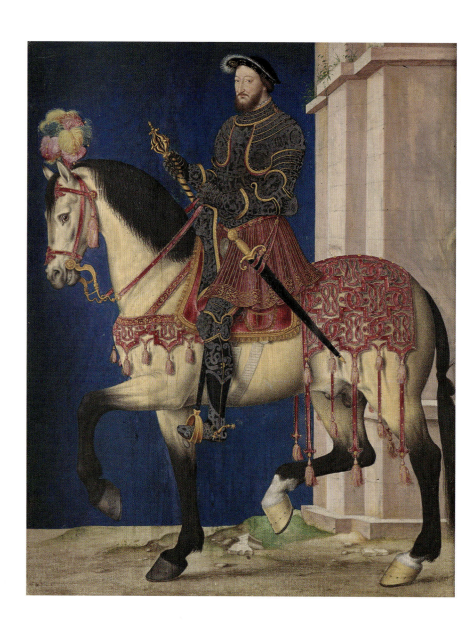

François Clouet (attrib.), *Francis I on Horseback, c.* 1540, miniature enhanced with gold by brush on parchment glued in full on panel.

Luxembourg to support William, his ally, but without much effect. In September William surrendered to Charles. The emperor pressed on, attacking Landrecies in the autumn. He hoped to draw Francis into action against him, but once more he was refused open battle.

Meanwhile, Hayre-ad-dîn had sailed once again into the Mediterranean as Süleyman had promised. In August 1543 his fleet attacked Nice – then an imperial vassal city – and Francis provided the port of Toulon, ordering it to be evacuated for the fleet's use. The Ottoman fleet spent the winter of 1543–4 there, to the scandal of Christendom. While a powerful force, in theory, it was not obvious how the fleet could best be deployed the following spring. Francis did not want to see it used directly against fellow Christians, but did not have the resources to sustain it, or indeed a clear strategic objective for it to achieve. This caused tension with the Ottomans, but they saw Francis as an ally worth maintaining. Hayre-ad-dîn finally withdrew in May, but not before he had forced Francis to pay him 800,000 crowns, apparently for the outfitting of the fleet. The Ottoman admiral then ravaged the west coast of Italy, taking some 6,000 people into slavery that summer, before returning to Istanbul in triumph at the end of what turned out to be his last maritime campaign.[16]

In the spring of 1543 Francis decided to make another direct effort to reclaim Milan, the third and final of his reign. A French army formed up within Piedmont, composed of French and Italian mounted troops and Swiss mercenaries, under the command of François de Bourbon, comte d'Enghien (1519–1546). In the spring of 1544, in what proved to be one of the last open encounters of the 'Italian Wars', at the Battle of Ceresole, Enghien defeated an army led by Alfonso d'Avalos d'Aquino (a cousin of the Marquis of Pescara who had defeated Francis in 1525; see Chapter Two). Blaise de Monluc was one of Enghien's infantry commanders. He noted in his memoirs that the battle had at first not gone well for the Swiss infantrymen, who met stiff resistance from veteran Spanish troops on the left wing of the French line. Rather as at Marignano, it took a series of cavalry charges, led by Enghien and costly in themselves, to repulse the Spanish, and the battle turned. Although such nobles as Monluc and Du Bellay celebrated Ceresole as a hard-won French victory, no invasion of Milan followed, and it made virtually no difference to Francis's strategic position in 1544.[17]

Meanwhile, Charles and Henry had agreed a more specific invasion plan against France. While Henry struck out from Calais and the Boulonnais with an army of 4,000 cavalry and 28,000 infantry, Charles would use his strong position in the northeast to attack France through Champagne. They would meet at the Marne, then converge on Paris with the combined forces of 60,000 men. In May, as agreed, Charles attacked through Champagne. Ferrante Gonzaga (1507–1557), the younger brother of Federico, who had spent time at the French court as a teenager, commanded for Charles. He had been appointed an imperial commander after the death of Bourbon in 1527 and defended Naples against Marshal Lautrec, and had been with Charles at Tunis in 1535. The Gonzaga were now firmly under the emperor's patronage. He took Luxembourg fairly easily, but was halted at Saint-Dizier on the Marne, which Francis had fortified. The king had also built defences along the southern bank of the river. It was several months before the fortress was taken.

In June 1544 the vanguard of the English army crossed to Calais, joining mercenary reinforcements there, and Henry himself arrived on 15 July. Ten days later the siege of Boulogne began in earnest under the king's personal command. In August Charles also took personal command of his army, advancing rapidly along the north bank of the Marne to a point beyond Châlons. His forces damaged villages and towns along their route, but his army could not ford the river. In a rather less heroic way, the Marne thus played in this invasion a defensive role akin to that of the Rhône in 1536. On 12 September Charles left the course of the river and turned northwest towards Soissons. He now planned to cross the Aisne river to rendezvous with his English ally's forces, which were expected by that time to have crossed the Somme. Henry, however, was mindful of the ill-fated dash towards Paris in 1523 in search of an imperial army that had never materialized. He had therefore determined first to secure Boulogne, remaining there until it was successfully taken in mid-September. By then, the emperor was running short of time, money and supplies, and welcomed Francis's insistent offers of a peace settlement. On 18 September, the day Henry entered Boulogne in triumph, a Franco-Imperial peace were signed at Crépy.[18]

The Franco-Habsburg settlement returned both sides to more or less the positions they had occupied under their entente of 1538, as amended by Charles's proposals in 1540. Once more, Orléans could eventually have the Netherlands instead of Milan if he married Charles's daughter Maria. Alternatively, he might possibly have Milan if he married Ferdinand's daughter Anna. It was Charles, not Francis, who was to make the decision between these alternatives. Less dramatic than Pavia it may have been, but it is hard not to see the war of 1542–4 as a kind of victory for Charles. It went some way towards repairing the damage done to his military reputation by his failed Provence campaign in 1536, and forced Francis once more to accept the terms Charles imposed upon him, including giving up a claim to Milan and with-drawing from Piedmont and Savoy. The king and his eldest son, Henri, were at odds, because the latter believed his father ought to have fought more vigorously for his interests in Milan. It also adversely affected Henri's relations with his younger brother Charles, whose position seemed to have been enhanced by the settlement at Crépy. Francis himself had gained nothing permanent by his actions, and at the end of the year he was again seriously ill. He had, however, at least defended his kingdom from the emperor, but he had lost a principal port town to Henry of England, the dauphin's efforts to retake the lower part of Boulogne having proved futile.

In the spring of 1545 Francis ordered naval operations against England, and began moving ships and their crews from the Mediterranean to supplement those in Norman and Breton ports. Monluc attributed Francis's campaign to the 'ardent desire the King had to revenge himself on the king of England'. So much was true, but his actions were primarily intended to disrupt the enemy's victualling and reinforcing of Boulogne. Henry's naval operations in the Narrow Sea had been complicated immensely by the demands of maintaining his conquest. During the summer, a force of approximately 30,000 infantry, together with companies of heavy cavalry raised in Normandy and Picardy, was assembled for action. A fleet of ships and galleys, estimated at about two-hundred-strong, was marshalled in the ports of Normandy, principally Le Havre. The objective seems to have been to seize one of England's southern coastal ports and hold it, if possible, as a bargaining chip for Boulogne. In cooperation with John Dudley, Lord Lisle (1504–1553), as Admiral, and Sir Francis Bryan (1490–1550), as Vice-Admiral, Henry responded with defensive operations at Portsmouth, Southampton and the Isle of Wight. The French fleet was commanded by Admiral Claude d'Annebault, who, although a reasonably able land commander, had no experience at sea. It sailed against England in mid-July, even if Annebault's flagship, *La Grande Maîtresse*, made an inauspicious start leading the fleet, running aground as it came out of the Seine.

Dudley's fleet was smaller than his enemy's – about 65 vessels, with more on the way from the West Country – but his were all fighting ships, and some of them quite large, even if most were still in port when the French arrived and began raiding the Sussex coast, the Isle of Wight and coastal towns near the Solent. The main engagement occurred on 19 July, when the French attempted to draw the English ships in the Solent into close action. In the course of this, the rebuilt *Mary Rose* under the command of Vice-Admiral Sir George Carew was turning about when she became unstable such that her gunports touched the water. Her crew had apparently failed to shut them after firing a salvo from that side against the French. That, and perhaps unevenly distributed weight on the vessel, then caused her to heel over completely and sink with the loss of nearly the whole crew – but this had no material effect on the sea battle itself. Although slow to get into meaningful action, the English eventually prevented any mainland invasion attempt and, over the course of the remainder of the summer, drove the French fleet off. Annebault was forced ignominiously to withdraw.[19]

With no money left on either side to continue the fight, a truce was reached in the autumn of 1545. After protracted negotiations, the Treaty of Ardres was finally signed on 7 June 1546 (26 years to the day after Francis had first met Henry at the Field of Cloth of Gold near the same town). The city of Boulogne was to remain in English possession for eight years. Thereafter it could be redeemed by Francis for 2 million crowns. It was perhaps the first Franco-English treaty of his reign that actively angered Francis. As his ambassadors explained, for Francis the English had 'brake the treaty first for that [they] gave not aid being asked, according to treaty'.[20] Despite the usual fulsome rhetoric with which it was ratified by both sides, the treaty contained no provision for any renewed 'eternal peace' of the kind first dreamed of by some at least in 1520. The English chronicler Edward Hall summed it up well: 'Although this peace pleased both the English and the French nations, yet surely both mistrusted the continuance of the same, considering the old proverb that what the eye sees, the heart rues.' Had both kings lived, it is likely that they would have been at war again before very long.[21]

The wars of 1542–5 were the longest and most expensive of Francis's reign. His outlay for them was twice that for the period 1536–8, and he built more fortifications in his last wars than in any previous ones, mainly for the defence of northern France. The wars also involved laying a number of sieges to imperial towns and withstanding sieges of French fortified places. Towns in the north had to be garrisoned and provisioned, in addition to the cost of raising and maintaining armies in the field. It has been estimated that the naval expedition against England in 1545 cost at least 2 million *livres*, and that of the whole period of war has been put at 30 million *livres*. Every expedient was used to raise revenue to meet such costs, overseen in good part by Tournon. These included increasing the *taille*, levying several *décimes* on the Church, taking forced loans from wealthy subjects, and having further recourse to commercial loans from Lyon and foreign bankers. The pressure of such financing had already led to a further overhaul of the fiscal administration by the Edict of Cognac in 1542. The kingdom was divided into sixteen financial administrative areas, the *recettes-général*, each overseen by a receiver, who collected all revenues. This essentially abolished revenue collection and disbursement according to the traditional distinction between 'ordinary' and 'extraordinary' income. The *receveurs-général* reported directly to the *Trésorier de l'Épargne*, who now had overall responsibility for the king's finances, vesting in the office the authority formerly exercised by the *gens des finances*. He answered directly to the king's council, thus cutting out another layer of management and, in theory at least, improving Francis's direct control over income he was owed, and his expenditure. Yet it never worked quite as well as intended. Although Francis had money in his coffers at his death, it was mostly all owed to bankers and, despite significant repayments, eighteen months into the reign of his successor, the debt was still almost 2.5 million *livres*.[22] His wars, of which he was so proud at the start of his reign, had proved very expensive indeed.

Epilogue:
'Le Grand Roi François'?

'Tis done! a father, mother, gone,
A sister, brother, torn away,
My hope is now in God alone,
Whom heaven and earth alike obey.
Above, beneath, to him is known, –
The world's wide compass is his own.
I love, – but in the world no more,
Nor in gay hall, or festal bower;
Not the fair forms I prized before.
MARGUERITE DE NAVARRE[1]

By the time the Treaty of Ardres was formally ratified in London and Paris in the summer of 1546, Francis had less than twelve months to live. Neither of the treaties signed with his enemies satisfied him. His major projects in the wake of the Anglo-Imperial invasion of 1543–4 were to fortify the northeastern frontier of his kingdom and to recover Boulogne earlier than had been agreed, either by negotiation or by force. His mood was not helped by his sons being at odds with each other. Francis once again had the prospect of Charles d'Orléans being recognized as duke of Milan under the Peace of Crépy, but that incensed the dauphin Henri, who formally protested against it, with some support from the *Parlement* of Paris.

Henri need not have worried about his younger brother usurping his position in regard to Milan. In September 1545 Charles died suddenly, aged only 23, of an unknown, perhaps viral, illness. With him went any prospect – however theoretical – of the restoration of the duchy of Milan to the Valois. Of Claude's seven children, only Henri and Marguerite now still lived.

In the latter part of 1545 Francis had also been called upon by his allies in the Schmalkaldic League for assistance against Charles V. Charles wanted to make the most of his military advantage and the peace treaty with Francis to turn his attention decisively against the League. A failed attempt to bring them back to the orthodox faith at the Council of Trent became the grounds for the emperor and the pope to work uneasily together planning a military campaign in Charles's German lands. The French regime's response to this situation was contradictory and rather ineffective. Francis wanted to assist the League but, financially stretched as he was, would commit funds only if Henry, too, committed himself to support the German Protestant princes and give the city of Boulogne to the League as guarantors for his performance of the terms of the Treaty of Ardres. In other words, Francis wanted to use the Germans to keep Henry honest. Henry had no money to offer, and in any case his affinity with the German Protestants had weakened markedly since 1540. While Madame d'Étampes, Marguerite de Navarre and Jean du Bellay were in favour of such support, Admiral Annebault and Cardinal Tournon advised against provoking the emperor by contravening the terms of the Peace of Crépy. During Annebault's visit to England in August 1546 to receive ratification of the Treaty of Ardres, Henry made the extraordinary suggestion to him that he and Francis had agreed 'within half a year' to abolish the Mass in England and France. This was news to Annebault. The suggestion was probably intended to sow dissent in French court circles by picking up on an idea about abolishing papal authority in France apparently put forward by Marguerite de Navarre and Madame d'Étampes earlier that year. The latter no longer favoured the religiously conservative admiral as she once had, and d'Étampes' last favourite, Nicolas de Bossut, comte de Longueval (d. ?1553), had been in contact with the king's secretary, Sir William Paget (1506–1563), and with Sir Nicholas Wotton (c. 1497–1567), then resident ambassador in France, about the idea. Paget steered clear of the whole subject, probably rightly, seeing the suggestion as part of a ruse to get Boulogne back ahead of time.[2] Francis eventually gave some financial aid to the Protestant princes, but it proved insufficient, and as early as the summer of 1546 the emperor declared war against the Elector of Saxony and Philip 1, Landgrave of Hesse (1504–1567). He began planning a decisive strike against them. Yet it was only with great difficulty that imperial troops were gathered from Spain, Naples, southern Germany and elsewhere for a campaign that culminated in the Battle of Mühlberg in April 1547.

By the start of 1547 Francis's health was beginning to fail. As was the case with his English counterpart, the effects of youthful injuries, especially those from hunting and his peripatetic lifestyle, became evident as he reached his fifties. While he never became obese as Henry did, Francis gained some weight and also seems to have been prone to relapses of the near-fatal (probably malarial) fever that he had first experienced in Spain in 1525. He also suffered from the effects of unspecified venereal disease. In early February the king learned of Henry's death on 28 January 1547, along with an apparent final admonition from his English rival to remember that he, too, was mortal. Yet, by late February Francis seemed to have recovered, and in early March he travelled, even hunted, via Madame d'Étampes' château of Limours to the southwest of Paris, arriving in the area of Rambouillet by the end of the month.

In the early weeks of March, however, his health again began to deteriorate rapidly. By 25 March all hope was lost that anything effective could be done for him. Henri was called to the king's side, and during the following few days Francis earnestly sought reconciliation with him. The two had often been distanced, but father and son were never fully estranged. Francis apparently urged his heir to repair some of the damage he feared he had done to his people through his wars and tax demands, and that to his reputation as a good Christian prince. Henri, too, seemed eager to be at one with Francis, even as he anticipated his own imminent accession. According to the account of Pierre du Chastel, the king's confessor and scholar-librarian, Francis sought absolution and heard Mass several times during the course of his last two days. Perhaps eager to show his master making a 'good death', Chastel recorded that the king's last word was 'Jesus'. King Francis I died at Rambouillet during the afternoon of Thursday, 31 March 1547. He was 52 years old.

Once Francis's death was confirmed, a form of post-mortem examination took place. The king had contracted venereal diseases in the course of his many and varied liaisons over the years. He is known to have been treated with mercury, the usual remedy for syphilis, although there is no evidence of his having symptoms, at his last, of the more advanced stages of that disease. According to a report sent to Francis's ally the duke of Ferrara, the king's brain, heart and liver were found to be healthy. Nevertheless, the debilitating effects of venereal infections in the form of abscesses on the urethra, together with damage to the lungs, intestines and kidneys, were evident.[3]

As soon as the king's death was made known, his close servants, who at that moment were effectively the court of France, acknowledged the new king, Henri II. He was the first Valois king since Louis XI to succeed his father directly and as an adult. He was also the last one to do so. As he established the core of his new regime, which included many of the minor members of the old one, the more prominent of his father's adherents were forced to give way. Chief among them was Madame d'Étampes, who had left for Limours two days before Francis's death. Her appointees were all dismissed from their court positions and she lost much, but not all, of the property and possessions given to her by the former king. She lived more than half her life after the death of Francis, and 'weathered the storm of disgrace remarkably effectively, carved for herself a new role and ended her life a moderately wealthy woman'.[4]

Within a very short time Henri II recalled Anne de Montmorency from internal exile. He joined the new king's council, was restored to all his offices and responsibilities, and was reimbursed for the salary he had forgone. The Constable and his affinity, alongside the heads of the Guise and Bourbon clans, now led the political nation under the king. In 1550 he was instrumental in negotiating the return of Boulogne from the English on good financial terms. Soon afterwards, Henri created him a duke and peer of France, and he exercised a powerful influence on government until the king's untimely death in 1559. Montmorency himself died in the course of the ensuing French Wars of Religion, of wounds suffered at the Battle of Saint-Denis in November 1567.

While the new regime began to organize, the former monarch's body was taken to the Priory of Haute-Bruyère, of the Order of Fontevrault, where the nuns kept vigil over it for several days. Then the heart, entrails and other vital organs were removed and the body embalmed. Later the heart was placed in an urn, designed by the sculptor Pierre Bontemps (c. 1505–1568), that remained at the priory until it was transferred to Saint-Denis in the nineteenth century. On 11 April the corpse was taken to the episcopal palace of Saint-Cloud. There, in the great hall and in accordance with royal funerary rites, a lifelike effigy of Francis, dressed in ceremonial robes and the collar of the Order of Saint-Michel, remained on display for eleven days. It was served meals and treated as if it were the king still alive. This complex funeral ritual was designed to uphold the constitutional fiction that the king of France never died, and to allow his successor time and space to put the essentials of his new regime in place, just as Francis had done at his own accession in 1515. In accordance with that ritual, the new monarch had no direct involvement in, nor was he present at, his predecessor's obsequies.

On 5 May the effigy was removed and Francis's coffin was placed on a catafalque in the great hall. There it remained for twelve days while funeral arrangements were completed. On 22 May a very large cortège, led by many senior clergy and leading nobles, escorted the coffin, mounted on a chariot, to Notre-Dame in Paris. After a short service there, it moved on to Saint-Denis, the royal mausoleum, the site of Queen Claude's coronation and her final resting place. On 24 May the coffin and, with it, those of Francis's two deceased sons were interred there. His household officers threw their wands into the grave. The point of the sword of state was briefly rested on the coffin and the banner of France was dipped into the grave to touch the coffin. The chief herald cried 'Le Roy est mort!' three times, then 'Vive le Roy!' The sword and banner were raised once more, and the beginning of the new reign and the continuity of French kingship were proclaimed.[5]

The tomb monument that commemorated Francis, his first queen and three of their children, the dauphin François, Charles d'Orléans and Princess Charlotte, was designed by Philibert de L'Orme (1510/15–1570). In Renaissance classical style, it resembles a triumphal arch but, in keeping with medieval tradition, it features effigies of the deceased at prayer above, and *gisants* (figures of their decaying bodies) below, carved by Bontemps. It also features bas-relief carvings of scenes of Francis's victory at Marignano in the opening year of his reign. One shows him charging in full armour, with couched lance, against a phalanx of Swiss pikemen, his artillery firing in the background. The tomb, which escaped the occasional iconoclastic fury of the Revolution, still

Tomb of Francis I and Claude de France, by Philibert de l'Orme, Basilica of Saint-Denis.

stands in Saint-Denis, not far from that of Francis's predecessor, Louis XII, and that of Henri II; it is a permanent memorial of the monarch who for some time after his death was known as 'Le Grand Roi, François'.

HOW GREAT, THEN, was Francis I as king of France? At times during his reign, this 'big boy', as Louis XII had called him in his youth, had indeed come close to ruining things, as Louis feared he might. He placed his kingdom in peril with his defeat in battle at Pavia in 1525. Yet, over the course of thirty years, he had also made France a force to be reckoned with as it had not quite been at his accession, and made his mark on its own internal history. Francis always wanted to rule as well as to reign. This determination to be obeyed, and his willingness to innovate in order to make the monarchy work as he wanted it to, led some twentieth-century historians to refer to him as a kind of 'proto-absolutist' monarch, whose authoritarian style anticipated that of the most famous king in French history: Louis XIV (1638–1715). More recent research, however, shows that the comparison needs significant qualification, and has affirmed that the monarchy of Francis I is rather better described as 'contractual', if authoritarian, than as 'absolutist'. Francis certainly exercised the spirit and letter of the royal prerogative to its fullest extent. He bargained hard over taxation, legal reform and religious orthodoxy as required with the provincial estates, the *parlements*, town councils, the clerical establishment and virtually every other interest group that declared itself, often by appearing not to bargain at all.[6]

If Francis I's monarchy was indeed 'contractual' in its approach, particularly to the nobility, it was undoubtedly through warfare, first and foremost, that the king sought to meet the terms of that contract, and to involve the nobility in projecting royal power within and beyond the French Renaissance state. For roughly

20 years of his 32 as king, Francis was at war, preparing for it, or actively managing its consequences in expensive and convoluted diplomacy. Shortly after his accession in 1515 he plunged into a decade of warfare that began in triumph but culminated in the loss of his prized duchy of Milan, and the decimation of the premier ranks of the *gendarmerie* at Pavia. The first round of the Valois–Habsburg wars finally ended only with the imposition of yet more financial burdens under the Treaty of Cambrai in 1529. Financially exhausted, even Francis had to stop fighting for a time. In the 1530s and 1540s he fought more effectively a defensive war against the emperor, with extensive fortifications, although he also lost Boulogne to Henry VIII. The king still gave his nobles ample opportunity to display their valour on the battlefield, even if the wars were astronomically expensive and did not bring quite the outcomes he hoped for. Historians have shown that the cost of war drove a concomitant tightening of decision-making in a smaller, more effective royal council under Francis, supported by a body of legal and financial specialists. It has also been shown how marked were the increase and creation for sale of judicial offices and the extension of an administrative network under him, but his recourse to *venalité* created problems of effective control over royal officers for his successors that lasted well into the following century.

Francis insisted on his prerogative at every turn and leaned heavily on the provincial estates, *parlements*, towns and cities, Lyon bankers, his own financial officials and highest courtiers, and above all the clergy for taxes, subsidies, forced loans and credit in general. He tried to get as much money out of as many people as possible, wherever he was and as often as he could, using all means available. Yet, for all the fiscal efficiencies, restructuring and administrative streamlining he oversaw, there is no evidence that Francis was driven by a doctrinaire desire for 'centralization' of government per se, as was once thought, but rather by his relentless personal ambitions and the crushing costs they regularly involved. His financial officials always struggled to get all the money he demanded into the central treasury of the *Épargne*, and were often made scapegoats for failings in the system.

The bulk of the revenue that was raised was spent, as one would expect, on the army, defence and debt, but a significant proportion was also spent on increasing the attractiveness of the royal court to the nobility, as part of Francis's efforts to recover and project once more the dynamic image of monarchy that had engendered such enthusiasm for him at his accession. More so than those of his predecessors and indeed his Valois successors, Francis I's court became large enough to serve his personal needs and to project such an image without being so big that it could not also function as the centre of a working royal affinity. Under Francis, the court and being at court – or at least being represented at court – mattered more than ever before.

One very important mechanism in attracting clients to direct royal service seems to have been the enhancement and clarification of the offices that gave regular access to the king, particularly that of *gentilhomme de la chambre du roi* – invented by Francis in 1515. The person who was largely (although never uniquely) responsible for appointments in the king's personal service for more than a decade from 1526 was Anne de Montmorency. His *clientele*, together with those of others linked to the royal circle, resulted, from the 1530s, in a network of contacts in the provinces below the level of the great dukes, built up under the king's aegis and control and unlike any that had existed in the same way before Francis's reign. It is to these years particularly that later sixteenth- and seventeenth-century commentators, such as Blaise de Monluc, Brantôme and Charles Loyseau in his *Cinq livres du droict des offices* (1613), looked back. They credited Francis not primarily with the administrative and judicial reforms so central to the 'absolutist' view of him, but rather for personally and effectively building up his court and attracting to it what Loyseau called 'men of great and noble houses', content to serve for small wages because of the prestige and opportunities it gave them, even if Loyseau at least also criticized him for allowing the provincial governors too much scope.[7] Admittedly looking back nostalgically from the perspective of the Wars of Religion and the collapse of royal authority, these writers also credited Francis with balancing – or at least appearing to balance – the ambitions of individuals and factions, and with containing without marginalizing the loyal magnates of the realm, chiefly the various branches of the Bourbon family after the Constable's revolt.[8]

Francis's character and personality have attracted criticism at times, especially from the nineteenth-century historians Jules Michelet and the Francophobic William Stubbs, who deplored the king's sexual appetites and the influence he allowed women in his regime. They also criticized him for arrogance and ingratitude towards his servants, especially those of lower social status. Some of this at least does find echoes in sixteenth-century critics. The king may well have thought that a court without women was like a garden without flowers, but Antonio de Beatis, who was in France in 1517 and made observations about Louise, also said of him that he 'breaks into other's gardens and drinks at many sources'.[9] Victor Hugo reinvigorated this view in his republican play Le Roi s'amuse (1832), which was not well received. Its plot is better known through Verdi's opera Rigoletto (1851), in which the character the Duke of Mantua is really Francis, a callous predator. Francis's relationships with women are sometimes still the subject of romantic or titillating gossip, especially online. More frequently these days, in serious scholarship at least, they are allowed more complexity and range. Those with his sister and mother, certainly, are seen far more positively than they once were, allowing the two women greater agency in their own right as noblewomen and key figures in his life, while censoriousness

Antoine Macault reading to the king and his courtiers, miniature from a 1534 French translation of Diodorus of Sicily's *Library of History*.

about his sex life otherwise is currently more muted – but that, too, may again change.

Francis's attitudes to religion have more recently found greater understanding, if not quite sympathy, among historians. His initial comparatively relaxed attitude towards debate and movements for reform, albeit within tightly controlled bounds at court, sit better with modern attitudes to religious debate, dissent and toleration. Yet he also sanctioned brutal suppression of the Vaudois in the south, even as he encouraged Ottoman action against the subjects of the emperor. He was also surprisingly ineffective against the spread of radical ideas, even after the clampdown on Sacramentarian dissent in the wake of the Affair of the Placards in 1534. There are interesting counter-factual questions to be posed about the extent to which Francis's failure to suppress dissent made his successor's task the greater, and how it contributed to the breakdown of religious and political consensus after Henri II's death – with tragic consequences for his kingdom and his dynasty, which was brought to a sudden end with the assassination of Francis's grandson Henri III (1551–1589).

It is now Francis's architectural, literary and artistic patronage that is regarded as his chief legacy, and that contributes most to his rather restored modern reputation. The years between 1529 and 1542 were ones of relative stability and prosperity, during which the king began most of the lasting administrative and legal reforms, and the artistic and architectural patronage, for which he is now mainly esteemed. The building and renovation of the principal châteaux at Fontainebleau, the Louvre, Saint-Germain-en-Laye, Amboise, Chambord, Blois and elsewhere were required to accommodate the increased scale of the court over which he presided, and to provide congenial public and private spaces where Francis's people could meet him, and one another, while also affording the king places of retreat and privacy. These residences, together with those of such courtiers as Montmorency and the Cardinal of Lorraine, and the major abbeys, also facilitated the king's frequent peregrinations around his kingdom, which continued until his last months. As the records of the royal itinerary, letters of weary ambassadors and the accounts of the *vénerie* and *fauconnerie* attest, Francis really did move out among his people throughout his reign, and he visited most parts of his kingdom either in war or in peace, usually hunting as he went.

Francis is perhaps second only to Henri IV (1553–1610) in his reputation for informality and spontaneity. He gave more entertainments in the 1530s than he had done during the first decade of his reign, but his court did not lack dignity. His residences were designed, built and decorated by the best talents available and showed Francis's genuine appreciation of artistic skill and endeavour, to a level of sophistication that is still outstanding among generations of French monarchs before and after him. His legacy to France in the works of Rosso Fiorentino, Francesco Primaticcio, the Clouets, Benvenuto Cellini and others, and his patronage of the foremost writers of his generation, anticipated the developments of the so-called *grand siècle*. In this respect at least, he does somewhat prefigure Louis XIV, who, like Francis, came to regret the expensive wars he began. Francis would have understood what Louis meant when he spoke of *le métier du roi*, the profession of kingship. The epithet 'Le Grand Roi' did not survive him that long, but if there is one monarch before Henri IV and Louis XIV whom the French still remember, and with some affection, it is Francis I.

REFERENCES

Introduction: Francis I, 'Renaissance' Monarch

1 Raphael Holinshed, *Chronicles of England, Scotland and Ireland 1587*, ed. Henry Ellis, 6 vols (London, 1807–8), vol. III, p. 611.

I *Le roi chevalier*

1 Abbé Lambert, ed., *Mémoires ou Journal de Louise de Savoie, duchesse d'Angoulesme etc., Collection universelle des memoires particuliers relatifs a l'histoire de France* (Paris, 1786), vol. XVI, p. 419.

2 Cédric Michon, 'Georges d'Amboise, principal conseiller de Louis XII', in *Georges d'Amboise 1460–1510: Une figure plurielle de la Renaissance*, ed. Jonathan Dumont and Laure Fagnart (Rennes, 2013), pp. 17–30.

3 Lambert, ed., *Mémoires ou Journal de Louise de Savoie*, vol. XVI, p. 411.

4 J. Brewer, J. Gairdner and R. H. Brodie, eds, *Letters and Papers, Foreign and Domestic of the Reign of Henry VIII, 1509–1547*, 21 vols and addenda (London, 1862–1932), vol. I, ii, 3342 (hereafter *LP*). All references are to item numbers, not pages.

5 Ernst Kantorowicz, *The King's Two Bodies* (Princeton, NJ, 1957); Ralph E. Giesey, *The Royal Funeral Ceremony in Renaissance France* (Geneva, 1960).

6 Baldassare Castiglione, *The Book of the Courtier* [1528], trans. George Bull (Harmondsworth, 1967), p. 88.

7 Myra Dickerman Orth, 'Francis de Moulin and the *Journal* of Louise of Savoy', *Sixteenth Century Journal*, XIII/1 (1982), pp. 55–66.

8 Glenn Richardson, 'Boys and Their Toys: Kingship, Masculinity and Material Culture in the Sixteenth Century', in *The Image and Perception of Monarchy in Medieval and Early Modern Europe*, ed. Sean McGlynn and Elena Woodacre (Newcastle upon Tyne, 2014), pp. 183–206.

9 Edward Hall, *The Union of the Two Noble and Illustre Famelies of York and Lancastre*, ed. Henry Ellis (London, 1809), p. 610; Morgan Prys,

'Un chroniqueur gallois à Calais', *Revue du Nord*, XLVII/185 (April–June 1965), pp. 195–202.

10   Anne was a male as well as female name in the sixteenth century.

11   Paul Marichal, ed., *Catalogue des actes de François Ier*, 10 vols (Paris, 1887–1910), vol. 1, 2, 7, 13, 43, 75, 100 (hereafter CAF; all references are to item numbers, not pages).

12   John Rigby Hale, ed., *The Travel Journal of Antonio de Beatis through Germany, Switzerland, the Low Countries, France and Italy, 1517–18* (London, 1979), pp. 107–8; Kathleen Wellman, *Queens and Mistresses of Renaissance France* (New Haven, CT, and London, 2013), p. 120.

13   Anne-Marie Lecoq, *François Ier: Imaginaire, symbolique et politique á l'aube de la Renaissance* (Paris, 1987), pp. 40–46.

14   Pierre de Vaissière, ed., *Journal de Jean Barrillon, secrétaire du chancelier Duprat, 1515–1521*, 2 vols (Paris, 1897–9), vol. 1, pp. 39–54.

15   Mack P. Holt, ed., *Renaissance and Reformation France* (Oxford, 2002), pp. 5–26.

16   *Ordonnances des rois de France: Règne de François Ier*, 9 vols (Paris, 1902–75), vol. 1, pp. 149–71.

17   CAF, vol. 1, 204, 216, 260–61.

18   Lecoq, *François Ier*, pp. 207–11.

19   Philippe Hamon and Jean Jacquart, *Archives de la France: Tome 3, Le XVIe siècle* (Paris, 1997), p. 179.

20   Père Anselme de Sainte-Marie, *Histoire généalogique et chronologique de la maison royale de France, des pairs, des grands officiers de la Couronne et de la Maison du Roy . . .*, 9 vols (Paris, 1726–33), vol. VIII, p. 502.

21   Ibid., pp. 721, 731.

22   David Potter, *Renaissance France at War: Armies, Culture and Society, c. 1480–1560* (Woodbridge, 2008), pp. 70–85.

23   Ibid., pp. 43–4, 70–85, 203–5.

24   Lecoq, *François Ier*, pp. 188–215.

25   CAF, vol. 1, 291, 311.

26   V. L. Bourrilly and F. Vindry, eds, *Mémoires de Martin et Guillaume du Bellay*, 4 vols (Paris, 1908–19), vol. 1, pp. 62–5.

27   Paolo Giovio, *La prima parte dell'istorie del suo tempo* (Venice, 1560), p. 460. Author's translation.

28   Alphonse Feillet, ed., *Histoire du gentil seigneur de Bayart, composée par le Loyal Serviteur* (Paris, 1867), pp. 351–4.

29   Ibid., p. 364.

30   François Demoulins, 'Commentaires de la guerre gallique', Bibliothèque Nationale de France, MS Français 13,429, f. 4b.

31 Louise de France died at just three years of age, on 21 September
    1517. Charlotte de France died a month before her eighth birthday
    in September 1524.
32 Demoulins, 'Commentaires', ff. 1–37.
33 Hale, ed., *Travel Journal*, p. 107.
34 Pierre de Boudeille, seigneur de Brantôme, *Vie de Claude de France*,
    www.corpusetampois.com accessed 15 January 2025.
35 Raffaele Tamalio, *Federico Gonzaga alla corte di Francesco I di Francia* (Paris,
    1994), pp. 149–54.
36 Ibid., p. 257; Wellman, *Queens and Mistresses*, pp. 124–30.
37 Christelle Cazaux, *La musique à la cour de François Ier* (Paris, 2002),
    pp. 20–65, 69–77, 126–39.
38 Barbara M. Stephenson, *The Power and Patronage of Marguerite de Navarre*
    (Aldershot, 2004), pp. 3–4, 189.
39 Halil Inalcik, *The Ottoman Empire: The Classical Age, 1300–1660* (London,
    2000), pp. 31–40.
40 *Ordonnances des rois*, vol. I, pp. 409ff.
41 Robert R. Harding, *Anatomy of a Power Elite: The Provincial Governors
    of Early Modern France* (New Haven, CT, and London, 1978),
    pp. 21–45.
42 Claude de Seyssel, *The Monarchy of France*, trans. J. H. Hexter,
    ed. D. Kelley (New Haven, CT, and London, 1984), pp. 14–58.
43 Robert J. Knecht, 'The Concordat of 1516: A Re-Assessment',
    in *Francis I and Sixteenth-Century France* (Farnham, 2015), pp. 16–32.
44 Glenn Richardson, *The Field of Cloth of Gold* (New Haven, CT, and
    London, 2013), pp. 23–37.
45 Janet Cox-Rearick, *Chefs d'œuvre de la Renaissance, la collection de François
    Ier* (Antwerp, 1995), pp. 207–11.
46 *LP*, vol. I, 3101, 3171.
47 Glenn Richardson, 'Entertainments for the French Ambassadors at
    the Court of Henry VIII', *Renaissance Studies*, IX/4 (1995), pp. 404–15.
48 Rawdon Brown, Cavendish Bentinck and Horatio Brown, eds,
    *Calendar of State Papers and Manuscripts Relating to English Affairs, Existing
    in the Archives and Collections of Venice etc.*, 9 vols (London, 1864–98),
    vol. II, p. 1287 (hereafter *CSP Ven.*); Glenn Richardson, 'The Privy
    Chamber of Henry VIII and Anglo-French Relations 1515–1520',
    Court Historian, IV/2 (1999), pp. 119–40.
49 *CSP Ven.*, vol. III, pp. 69, 54.
50 Richardson, *The Field of Cloth of Gold*, pp. 38–72.
51 Ibid., pp. 101–40.

52 Robert Goubaux and Paul-André Lemoisne, eds, *Mémoires du Maréchal de Florange* (Paris, 1924), vol. II, pp. 268–70; *CSP Ven.*, vol. III, pp. 50, 90, Soardino to the Marquess of Mantua; p. 91, Giovanni Badoer and Antonio Giustiniani to the Venetian Signory. Ibid.

53 *CSP Ven.*, vol. II, p. 90, Soardino to the Marquess of Mantua, 'Lisien' [Licques], 19 June 1520. My italics.

2 A Kingdom in the Hazard

 1 Aimé Champollion-Figeac, ed., *Captivité du roi François Ier* (Paris, 1847), p. 129.

 2 In January 1537 Madeleine was married to James V of Scotland.

 3 Pierre de Vaissière, ed., *Journal de Jean Barrillon, secrétaire du chancelier Duprat, 1515–1521*, 2 vols (Paris, 1897–9), vol. II, p. 176; *LP*, vol. III, i, 1161, 1183. English ambassadors were reporting the king's injury and recovery by late February.

 4 On the details of Charles's entertainment in England, see Sydney Anglo, *Spectacle, Pageantry and Early Tudor Policy* (Oxford, 1969), pp. 179–206.

 5 Robert J. Knecht, *Renaissance Warrior and Patron: The Reign of Francis I* (Cambridge, 1994), pp. 201–9.

 6 *LP*, vol. IV, 365, 374.

 7 A. Feillet, ed., *Histoire du gentil seigneur de Bayart, composée par le Loyal Serviteur* (Paris, 1867), pp. 335–43.

 8 *LP*, vol. IV, 789, 826, 837.

 9 Ibid., 780.

10 Angus Konstam, *Pavia 1525: The Climax of the Italian Wars* (Oxford, 1996), p. 81.

11 Paolo Giovio, *La vita del signor Don Ferrando Davalo, Marchese di Pescara* (Florence, 1556), p. 118.

12 Ibid.

13 *LP*, vol. IV, 1212.

14 Jack J. Scarisbrick, *Henry VIII* (London, 1968), pp. 135–45. Geoffrey Parker, *Emperor: A New Life of Charles V* (New Haven, CT, and London, 2019), pp. 141–8.

15 Champollion-Figeac, ed., *Captivité*, p. 100.

16 Ibid., pp. 476–7.

17 *LP*, vol. IV, 2148, 1956, 1967; Parker, *Emperor*, pp. 149–56.

18 Louis Lalanne, ed., *Journal d'un bourgeois de Paris sous le règne de François Ier, 1515–1536* (Paris, 1854), pp. 297–300.

19 Parker, *Emperor*, p. 167.
20 *LP*, vol. IV, i, 2148, 1956, 1967; Parker, *Emperor*, pp. 149–56.
21 *LP*, vol. IV, ii, 3080; *CAF*, vol. IV, 2657.
22 Glenn Richardson, *Wolsey* (New Haven, CT, and London, 2020), pp. 192–218.
23 Joycelyne G. Russell, *Diplomats at Work: Three Renaissance Studies* (Stroud, 1992), pp. 94–152.
24 Quoted in Dorothy M. Mayer, *The Great Regent: Louise de Savoy, 1476–1531* (London, 1966), p. 293: 'Qui avez triomphe du malheur triumphant; En saulvant notre honneur, paix, et votre enfant; En guerre soustenant, avec la paix reduite; Par vostre grand vertu, et tres sage conduite.'

3 Francis as Governor and Patron

1 Pierre de Bourdeille, seigneur de Brantôme, *Œuvres complètes*, ed. Ludovic Lalanne, 11 vols (Paris, 1864–82), vol. II, p. 118.
2 Thierry Rentet, 'Network Mapping: Ties of Fidelity and Dependency among the Major Domestic Officers of Anne de Montmorency', *French History*, XVII/2 (2003), pp. 109–26.
3 Bibliothèque Nationale de France, MS Français 21,449, ff. 129r–30v. MS Français 21,450, ff. 96r–97v for a list of *gentilshommes* for 1546, the last full year of Francis I's life. The figure of 50 excludes five unsalaried 'autres gentilshommes'.
4 Robert R. Harding, *Anatomy of a Power Elite: The Provincial Governors of Early Modern France* (New Haven, CT, and London, 1978), p. 27.
5 Mark Greengrass, 'Property and Politics in Sixteenth-Century France: The Landed Fortune of Constable Anne de Montmorency', *French History*, II/4 (1988), pp. 371–98.
6 Bibliothèque Nationale de France, MS Français 21,450, f. 3v.
7 Malcolm Walsby, *The Counts of Laval: Culture, Patronage and Religion in Fifteenth- and Sixteenth-Century France* (Aldershot, 2007), pp. 90–93. Montmorency was also involved in a successful attempt by a cadet branch of the Rohan family to join with the main branch of the Lavals, and in 1529 he oversaw the placement as a *gentilhomme de la chambre* of Louis V de Rohan-Guéméné, who married Guy XVI's daughter Marguerite and joined the inner circle of his affinity.
8 David Potter, *War and Government in the French Provinces: Picardy, 1470–1560* (Cambridge, 1993), pp. 72–6; see also Harding, *Anatomy of a Power Elite*, p. 226.
9 Potter, *War and Government*, pp. 137–8.

10 Monique Chatenet, *La Cour de France au XVIe siècle: Vie sociale et architecture* (Paris, 2002), pp. 71–2; Robert J. Knecht, 'Francis I and Paris', *History*, LXVI/216 (1981), pp. 18–33.

11 Jean-Pierre Babelon, *Châteaux de France au siècle de la Renaissance* (Paris, 1989), pp. 318–23.

12 Monique Chatenet, *Le Château de Madrid au Bois de Boulogne* (Paris, 2000); *The Diary of John Evelyn*, ed. E. S. De Beer, selections by Roy Strong (Oxford, 2006), pp. 63, 253.

13 Raffaele Tamalio, *Federico Gonzaga alla corte di Francesco I di Francia* (Paris, 1994), pp. 287–90, 292–3.

14 Niccolò Tommaseo, *Relations des ambassadeurs vénitiens sur les affaires de France*, 2 vols (Paris, 1838), vol. I, pp. 28–9.

15 Mary Hollingsworth, *The Cardinal's Hat: Money, Ambition and Housekeeping in a Renaissance Court* (London, 2004), p. 50.

16 Ibid., pp. 120–21, 213.

17 *The Diary of John Evelyn*, ed. De Beer, pp. 222–3.

18 Peter Mellen, *Jean Clouet* (London, 1971), pp. 47ff; Janet Cox-Rearick, *Chefs d'œuvre de la Renaissance: La Collection de François Ier* (Antwerp, 1995), pp. 7–9.

19 For a copy and variation of the Titian portrait at Harewood House and in Oslo, see Cox-Rearick, *Chefs d'œuvre*, pp. 248–51.

20 Sophie Schneebalg-Perelman, 'Richesses du garde-meuble parisien de François Ier, inventaires inédits de 1542 et 1551', *Gazette des Beaux-Arts*, LXXVIII (1971), pp. 253–304.

21 Archives Nationales de France, MS Series J947, no. 3, ff. 1r–4r, an inventory of gemstones and their settings, Paris, February 1533; Michèle Bimbenet-Privat, *Les orfèvres parisiens de la Renaissance (1506–1620)* (Paris, 1992), pp. 245–7, 508, 545; Ilaria Toesca, 'Silver in the Time of Francois Ier: A New Identification', *Apollo*, XC (October 1969), pp. 292–7.

22 Philippe Hamon, *L'Argent du roi: Les finances sous François Ier* (Paris, 1994), pp. 45–85.

23 Ibid., pp. 66–96; Potter, *War and Government*, pp. 250–53.

24 Hamon, *L'Argent du roi*, pp. 94ff.

25 Ibid., pp. 257–63.

26 Ibid., pp. 293–301.

27 Nicole Lemaitre, 'Les Évêques réformateurs français et leur personnel dans le choc de la Réformation luthérienne (1523–1529)', in *François Ier et Henri VIII: Deux Princes de la Renaissance (1515–1547)*, ed. Charles Giry-Deloison (Lille, 1996), pp. 103–19.

28 Robert J. Knecht, 'Francis I, "Defender of the Faith"', in *Francis I and Sixteenth-Century France* (Farnham, 2015), part IX, pp. 106–27.

29 Brantôme, *Œuvres complètes*, vol. IX, p. 272; *LP*, vol. VI, 892, Duke of Norfolk to Henry VIII, June 1533.

30 Marie-Ange Boitel-Souriac, 'Quand Vertu vient de l'étude des bonnes lettres: L'Éducation humaniste des enfants de France de François Ier aux derniers Valois', *Revue Historique*, CCCX/1 (2008), pp. 33–59.

31 *State Papers Published under the Authority of His Majesty's Commission, King Henry VIII*, 11 vols (London, 1830–52), vol. VII, p. 891, Bryan to Henry VIII, Paris, 23 March 1531.

32 Pierre de Bourdeille, seigneur de Brantôme, *Vie des dames galantes*, ed. H. Vigneau (Paris, 1857).

33 Giorgio Vasari, *The Lives of the Artists*, trans. Julia Conaway Bondanella and Peter Bondanella (Oxford, 1991), p. 354.

34 Robert J. Knecht, 'Francis I and Fontainebleau', *Court Historian*, IV/2 (1999), pp. 93–118.

35 Ibid.

36 Sylvie Béguin, Jean Guillaume and Alain Roy, eds, *La Galerie d'Ulysse à Fontainebleau* (Paris, 1985), pp. 9–42.

37 Babelon, *Châteaux de France*, pp. 162–3; *The Diary of John Evelyn*, ed. De Beer, p. 77. Molière's *Le Bourgeois gentilhomme*, with music by Jean-Baptiste Lully, was premiered before Louis XIV at Chambord on 14 October 1670.

38 Cox-Rearick, *Chefs d'œuvre*, pp. 325–37; Cécile Scailliérez, *François Ier et ses artistes dans les collections du Louvre* (Paris, 1992), pp. 124–5.

39 Caroline Elam, 'Art in the Service of Liberty: Battista della Palla, Art Agent for Francis I', *I Tatti Studies in the Italian Renaissance*, V (1993), pp. 33–109.

40 Cox-Rearick, *Chefs d'œuvre*, pp. 288–94, 392–6; Benvenuto Cellini, *Autobiography*, trans. George Bull (London, 1998), pp. 251–310.

41 *CAF*, vol. I, 527; Marian Rothstein, 'Homer for the Court of François I', *Renaissance Quarterly*, LIX/3 (2006), pp. 732–67.

42 Musée Condé, MS 721.

43 See '*Journal officiel* de la République française', www.legifrance.gouv.fr, accessed 10 December 2024, for the text of the Ordonnance.

44 Hélène J. Harvitt, 'Hugues Salel, Poet and Translator', *Modern Philology*, XVI/11 (March 1919), pp. 155–65.

4 The Warrior Again

1   Blaise de Monluc, *The Commentaries of Messire Blaize de Monluc, Mareschal of France*, trans. Charles Cotton (London, 1674), book VII, p. 404.

2   Glenn Richardson, 'The French Connection: Francis I and England's Break with Rome', in *'The Contending Kingdoms': France and England, 1420–1700*, ed. Glenn Richardson (Aldershot, 2008), pp. 95–116.

3   V. L. Bourrilly and F. Vindry, eds, *Mémoires de Martin et Guillaume du Bellay*, 4 vols (Paris, 1908–19), vol. II, p. 299.

4   Geoffrey Parker, *Emperor: A New Life of Charles V* (New Haven, CT, and London, 2019), p. 256.

5   Xavier Le Person, 'A Moment of "Resverie": Charles V and Francis I's Encounter at Aigues-Mortes (July 1538)', *French History*, XIX/1 (2005), pp. 1–27.

6   Robert J. Knecht, *Renaissance Warrior and Patron: The Reign of Francis I* (Cambridge, 1994), pp. 385–97.

7   Charles Weiss, ed., *Papiers d'état du Cardinal de Granvelle*, 9 vols (Paris, 1841–52), vol. II, pp. 540–42, letter dated October 1539.

8   Thierry Rentet, *Anne de Montmorency, Grand Maître de François Ier* (Rennes, 2011), pp. 147–78, 383–90.

9   Parker, *Emperor*, pp. 266–8.

10 Ibid., p. 267.

11 Richard W. Hoyle and John B. Ramsdale, 'The Royal Progress of 1541, the North of England, and Anglo-Scottish Relations, 1534–42', *Northern History*, XLI/2 (September 2004), pp. 239–65.

12 Knecht, *Renaissance Warrior*, pp. 395–7.

13 François Nawrocki, *L'Amiral Claude d'Annebault, conseiller favori de François Ier* (Paris, 2015).

14 Cédric Michon, 'Conseils et conseillers en France (1461–1547)', in *Conseils et conseillers dans l'Europe de la Renaissance v. 1450–1550*, ed. Cédric Michon (Rennes, 2012), pp. 89–108.

15 Cédric Michon, 'Le Cardinal Jean du Bellay et ses bénéfices en France sous François Ier et Henri II', in *Le Cardinal Jean du Bellay: diplomatie et culture dans l'Europe de la Renaissance*, ed. Cédric Michon and Loris Petris (Rennes, 2013), pp. 67–88.

16 Nicolas Vatin, 'The Ottoman View of France from the Late Fifteenth to the Mid-Sixteenth Century', *French History*, XXIX/10 (2015), pp. 6–11.

17 David Potter, *Renaissance France at War: Armies, Culture and Society, c. 1480–1560* (Woodbridge, 2008), pp. 189–90.

18 Neil Murphy, 'Violence, Colonisation and Henry VIII's Conquest of France 1544–1546', *Past and Present*, CCXXXIII/1 (November 2016), pp. 13–51.
19 Geoffrey Moorhouse, *Great Harry's Navy: How Henry VIII Gave England Sea Power* (London, 2005), pp. 243–63.
20 *LP*, vol. XXI, i, 1014; G. A. Bergenroth et al., eds, *Calendar of State Papers, Spanish*, 13 vols (London, 1862–1964), vol. VIII, 279. References are to item numbers, not page numbers.
21 Edward Hall, *The Union of the Two Noble and Illustre Famelies of York and Lancastre*, ed. Henry Ellis (London, 1809), p. 867.
22 Philippe Hamon, *L'Argent du roi: Les finances sous François Ier* (Paris, 1994), pp. 31–48, 261–3, 554–5.

Epilogue: 'Le Grand Roi François'?

1 Bliss Carman et al., eds, *The World's Best Poetry* (Philadelphia, PA, 1904), available at www.bartleby.com, accessed 2 September 2024.
2 David Potter, 'Politics and Faction at the Court of Francis I: The Duchesse d'Étampes, Montmorency and the Dauphin Henri', *French History*, XXI/2 (2007), pp. 127–46.
3 David Potter, 'La Fin du règne de François Ier et l'avènement d'Henri II d'après les dèpêches de Jean de Saint-Mauris (1547)', Cour de France, article 2749, www.cour-de-france.fr, accessed 10 December 2024.
4 David Potter, 'The Life and After-Life of a Royal Mistress: Anne de Pisseleu, Duchess of Étampes', in *Women and Power at the French Court, 1483–1563*, ed. Susan Broomhall (Amsterdam, 2018), pp. 309–34.
5 Ralph E. Giesey, *The Royal Funeral Ceremony in Renaissance France* (Geneva, 1960), pp. 1–17, 193–5.
6 Roseline Claerr and Olivier Poncet, *La prise de décision en France (1525–1559)* (Paris, 2008).
7 Charles Loyseau, *Cinq Livres du droict des offices, avec le livre des seigneuries et celui des ordres* (Paris, 1649), pp. 426–9.
8 Paul Dognon, *Les Institutions politiques et administratives du pays de Languedoc du XIIIe siècle aux guerres de religion* (Toulouse, 1896), p. 491. Dognon emphasized the strength of local tradition in the face of royal demands well beyond the reign of Francis I.
9 John Rigby Hale, ed., *The Travel Journal of Antonio de Beatis through Germany, Switzerland, the Low Countries, France and Italy, 1517–18* (London, 1979), p. 107.

SELECT BIBLIOGRAPHY

Manuscript sources

Archives Nationales de France, Paris: MS Series J947
Bibliothèque Nationale de France, Paris: François Demoulins,
'Commentaires de la guerre gallique', MS français 13,429; MS français
21,449; 21,450.
Musée Condé, Chantilly: MS 721.

Printed primary sources

Anselme de Sainte-Marie, Père, *Histoire généalogique et chronologique
de la maison royale de France . . .*, 9 vols (Paris, 1726–33)
Bergenroth, G. A., et al., eds, *Calendar of State Papers, Spanish*, 13 vols
(London, 1862–1964)
Bourdeille, Pierre de, seigneur de Brantôme, *Œuvres complètes*, ed. Ludovic
Lalanne, 11 vols (Paris, 1864–82)
Bourrilly, V. L., and F. Vindry, eds, *Mémoires de Martin et Guillaume du Bellay*,
4 vols (Paris, 1908–19)
Brantôme, Pierre de Boudeille, seigneur de, *Vie des dames galantes*,
ed. H. Vigneau (Paris, 1857)
—, *Œuvres complètes*, ed. Ludovic Lalanne, 11 vols (Paris, 1864–82)
—, *Vie de Claude de France*, www.corpusetampois.com, accessed
15 January 2025
Brewer, J., James Gairdner and R. H. Brodie, eds, *Letters and Papers, Foreign
and Domestic of the Reign of Henry VIII, 1509–1547*, 21 vols and addenda
(London, 1862–1932)
Brown, Rawdon, trans., *Four Years at the Court of Henry VIII. Selection
of Despatches Written by the Venetian Ambassador Sebastian Giustinian . . .
1515 to 1519*, 2 vols (London, 1854)
—, Cavendish Bentinck and Horatio Brown, eds, *Calendar of State*

Papers and Manuscripts Relating to English Affairs, Existing in the Archives and Collections of Venice etc., 9 vols (London, 1864–98)

Castiglione, Baldassare, *The Book of the Courtier* [1528], trans. George Bull (Harmondsworth, 1967)

Cellini, Benvenuto, *Autobiography*, trans. George Bull (London, 1998)

De Beer, E. S., ed., *The Diary of John Evelyn*, selections by Roy Strong (Oxford, 2006)

Feillet, Alphonse, ed., *Histoire du gentil seigneur de Bayart, composée par le Loyal Serviteur* (Paris, 1867)

Giovio, Paolo, *La vita del signor Don Ferrando Davalo, Marchese di Pescara* (Florence, 1556)

—, *La prima parte dell'istorie del suo tempo* (Venice, 1560)

Goubaux, Robert, and Paul-André Lemoisne, eds, *Mémoires du Maréchal de Florange*, 2 vols (Paris, 1913, 1924)

Hale, John Rigby, ed., *The Travel Journal of Antonio de Beatis through Germany, Switzerland, the Low Countries, France and Italy, 1517–18* (London, 1979)

Hall, Edward, *The Union of the Two Noble and Illustre Famelies of York and Lancastre*, ed. Henry Ellis (London, 1809)

Hinds, Allen B., ed., *Calendar of State Papers and Manuscripts in the Archives and Collections of Milan, 1385–1618* (London, 1912)

Holinshed, Raphael, *Chronicles of England, Scotland and Ireland 1587*, ed. Henry Ellis, 6 vols (London, 1807–8)

Lalanne, Louis, ed., *Journal d'un bourgeois de Paris sous le règne de François Ier, 1515–1536* (Paris, 1854)

Lambert, Abbé, ed., *Mémoires ou Journal de Louise de Savoie, duchesse d'Angoulesme etc., collection universelle des memoires particuliers relatifs a l'histoire de France*, vol. XVI (Paris, 1786)

Loyseau, Charles, *Cinq Livres du droict des offices, avec le livre des seigneuries et celui des ordres* (Paris, 1649)

Marichal, Paul, ed., *Catalogue des actes de François Ier*, 10 vols (Paris, 1887–1910)

Monluc, Blaise de, *The Commentaries of Messire Blaize de Monluc, Mareschal of France*, trans. Charles Cotton (London, 1674)

Ordonnances des rois de France: Règne de François Ier, 9 vols (Paris, 1902–75)

Orth, Myra D., 'Francis de Moulin and the *Journal* of Louise of Savoy', *Sixteenth Century Journal*, XIII/1 (1982), pp. 55–66

Pace, Richard, *Oratio Ricardii Pacei in pace nuperrime composita* (London, 1518)

Rymer, Thomas, ed., *Foedera, conventiones, literae et cuiuscunque generic acta publica*, 20 vols (London, 1727–35)

Seyssel, Claude de, *The Monarchy of France*, trans. J. H. Hexter,
    ed. D. Kelley (New Haven, CT, and London, 1984)
*State Papers Published under the Authority of His Majesty's Commission,
    King Henry VIII*, 11 vols (London, 1830–52)
Tamalio, Raffaele, *Federico Gonzaga alla corte de Francesco I di Francia*
    (Paris, 1994)
Tommaseo, Niccolò, *Relations des ambassadeurs vénitiens sur les affaires de France*,
    2 vols (Paris, 1838)
Vaissière, Pierre de, ed., *Journal de Jean Barrillon, secrétaire du chancelier Duprat*,
    1515–1521, 2 vols (Paris, 1897–9)
Vasari, Giorgio, *The Lives of the Artists*, trans. Julia Conaway Bondanella
    and Peter Bondanella (Oxford, 1991)
Weiss, Charles, ed., *Papiers d'état du Cardinal de Granvelle*, 9 vols (Paris,
    1841–52)

Secondary sources: books and articles

Anglo, Sydney, *Spectacle, Pageantry and Early Tudor Policy* (Oxford, 1969)
Babelon, Jean-Pierre, *Châteaux de France au siècle de la Renaissance* (Paris,
    1989)
Baumgartner, Frederic J., *Louis XII* (Basingstoke, 1996)
Béguin, Sylvie, Jean Guillaume and Alain Roy, eds, *La Galerie
    d'Ulysse à Fontainebleau* (Paris, 1985)
Bimbenet-Privat, Michèle, *Les orfèvres Parisiens de la Renaissance
    (1506–1620)* (Paris, 1992)
Boitel-Souriac, Marie-Ange, 'Quand Vertu vient de l'étude
    des bonnes lettres: L'Éducation humaniste des enfants de
    France de François Ier aux derniers Valois', *Revue Historique*,
    CCCX/1 (2008), pp. 33–59
Carman, Bliss, et al., eds, *The World's Best Poetry* (Philadelphia,
    PA, 1904), available at www.bartleby.com, accessed 2 September
    2024
Carouge, Pierre, 'Artus (1474–1519) et Guillaume (1482–1525)
    Gouffier à l'émergence de nouvelles modalities de gouvernement',
    in *Les Conseillers de François Ier*, ed. Cédric Michon (Rennes, 2011),
    pp. 229–53
Cazaux, Christelle, *La Musique à la cour de François Ier* (Paris, 2002)
Chambers, David, and Jane Martineau, *Splendours of the Gonzaga*,
    exh. cat., Victoria and Albert Museum, London (1981)
Champollion-Figeac, Aimé, ed., *Captivité du roi François Ier* (Paris, 1847)

Charton-Le Clech, Sylvie, *Chancellerie et culture au xvie siècle: Les notaires et secrétaires du roi de 1515 à 1547* (Toulouse, 1993)

Chatenet, Monique, *Le Château de Madrid au Bois de Boulogne* (Paris, 2000)

—, *La cour de France au xvie siècle: Vie sociale et architecture* (Paris, 2002)

Claerr, Roseline, and Olivier Poncet, *La prise de décision en France (1525–1559)* (Paris, 2008)

Cox-Rearick, Janet, *Chefs d'œuvre de la Renaissance: La collection de François Ier* (Antwerp, 1995)

—, *The Collection of Francis I: Royal Treasures* (Antwerp, 1995)

Crawford, Katherine B., *The Sexual Culture of the French Renaissance* (Cambridge, 2010)

Dognon, Paul, *Les Institutions politiques et administratives du pays de Languedoc du XIIIe siècle aux guerres de religion* (Toulouse, 1896)

Elam, Caroline, 'Art in the Service of Liberty: Battista della Palla, Art Agent for Francis I', *I Tatti Studies in the Italian Renaissance*, v (1993), pp. 33–109

Giesey, Ralph E., *The Royal Funeral Ceremony in Renaissance France* (Geneva, 1960)

Greengrass, Mark, 'Property and Politics in Sixteenth-Century France: The Landed Fortune of Constable Anne de Montmorency', *French History*, II/4 (1988), pp. 371–98

Gunn, S. J., 'The Duke of Suffolk's March on Paris in 1523', *English Historical Review*, CI/400 (1986), pp. 596–634

Gwyn, Peter, 'Wolsey's Foreign Policy: The Conferences at Calais and Bruges Reconsidered', *Historical Journal*, XXIII/4 (1980), pp. 755–72

Hamon, Philippe, *L'Argent du roi: Les finances sous François Ier* (Paris, 1994)

—, 'Semblançay homme de finances et de Conseil (c. 1455–1527)', in Michon, ed., *Les Conseillers*, pp. 117–30

—, and Jean Jacquart, *Archives de la France: Tome 3, Le XVIe siècle* (Paris, 1997)

Harding, Robert R., *Anatomy of a Power Elite: The Provincial Governors of Early Modern France* (New Haven, CT, and London, 1978)

Harvitt, Hélène J., 'Hugues Salel, Poet and Translator', *Modern Philology*, XVI/11 (March 1919), pp. 155–65

Hollingsworth, Mary, *The Cardinal's Hat: Money, Ambition and Housekeeping in a Renaissance Court* (London, 2004)

Holt, Mack P., ed., *Renaissance and Reformation France* (Oxford, 2002)

Hoyle, Richard W., and John B. Ramsdale, 'The Royal Progress of 1541, the North of England, and Anglo-Scottish Relations, 1534–42', *Northern History*, XLI/2 (September 2004), pp. 239–65

Inalcik, Halil, *The Ottoman Empire: The Classical Age, 1300–1660* (London, 2000)

Kantorowicz, Ernst, *The King's Two Bodies* (Princeton, NJ, 1957)

Knecht, Robert J., *Renaissance Warrior and Patron: The Reign of Francis I* (Cambridge, 1994)

—, 'Francis I and Fontainebleau', *Court Historian*, IV/2 (1999), pp. 93–118

—, *The French Renaissance Court* (New Haven, CT, and London, 2008)

—, 'Jacques II de Chabannes, seigneur de La Palisse ou La Palice (v. 1470–1525)', in Michon, ed., *Les Conseillers*, pp. 163–70

—, 'Jacques de Genouillac dit Galiot (v. 1465–1546)', in Michon, ed., *Les Conseillers*, pp. 155–61

—, *Francis I and Sixteenth-Century France* (Farnham, 2015)

Konstam, Angus, *Pavia 1525: The Climax of the Italian Wars* (Oxford, 1996)

Lecoq, Anne-Marie, *François Ier: Imaginaire, symbolique et politique á l'aube de la Renaissance* (Paris, 1987)

Lemaitre, Nicole, 'Les Évêques réformateurs français et leur personnel dans le choc de la Réformation luthérienne (1523–1529)', in *François Ier et Henri VIII: Deux Princes de la Renaissance (1515–1547)*, ed. Charles Giry-Deloison (Lille, 1996), pp. 103–19

Le Person, Xavier, 'A Moment of "Resverie": Charles V and Francis I's Encounter at Aigues-Mortes (July 1538)', *French History*, XIX/1 (2005), pp. 1–27

Mayer, Dorothy M., *The Great Regent, Louise de Savoy* (London, 1966)

Mellen, Peter, *Jean Clouet* (London, 1971)

Michon, Cédric, ed., *Les Conseillers de François Ier* (Rennes, 2011)

—, ed., *Conseils et conseillers dans l'Europe de la Renaissance v. 1450–1550* (Rennes, 2012)

—, 'Le Cardinal Jean du Bellay et ses bénéfices en France sous François Ier et Henri II', in *Le Cardinal Jean du Bellay: Diplomatie et culture dans l'Europe de la Renaissance*, ed. Cédric Michon and Loris Petris (Rennes, 2013), pp. 67–88

—, 'Georges d'Amboise, principal conseiller de Louis XII', in *Georges d'Amboise 1460–1510: Une figure plurielle de la Renaissance*, ed. Jonathan Dumont and Laure Fagnart (Rennes, 2013), pp. 17–30

Moorhouse, Geoffrey, *Great Harry's Navy: How Henry VIII Gave England Sea Power* (London, 2005)

Murphy, Neil, 'Violence, Colonisation and Henry VIII's Conquest of France 1544–1546', *Past and Present*, CCXXXIII/1 (November 2016), pp. 13–51

Nawrocki, François, *L'Amiral Claude d'Annebault, conseiller favori de François Ier* (Paris, 2015)

Orth, Myra Dickerman, 'Francis de Moulin and the *Journal* of Louise of
    Savoy', *Sixteenth Century Journal*, XIII/1 (1982), pp. 55–66
Parker, Geoffrey, *Emperor: A New Life of Charles V* (New Haven, CT, and
    London, 2019)
Pérouse de Montclos, Jean-Marie, *Fontainebleau* (New York, 1998)
Potter, David L., *War and Government in the French Provinces: Picardy, 1470–1560*
    (Cambridge, 1993)
—, *A History of France, 1460–1560: The Emergence of a Nation State* (Basingstoke,
    1995)
—, 'Politics and Faction at the Court of Francis I: The Duchesse
    d'Étampes, Montmorency and the Dauphin Henri', *French History*,
    XXI/2 (2007), pp. 127–46
—, *Renaissance France at War: Armies, Culture and Society, c. 1480–1560*
    (Woodbridge, 2008)
—, 'Ages to the Renaissance: The Development of a Political Culture',
    Cour de France (2011), article 1883, www.cour-de-france.fr,
    accessed 10 December 2024
—, 'The Life and After-Life of a Royal Mistress: Anne de Pisselieu,
    Duchess of Étampes', in *Women and Power at the French Court, 1483–1563*,
    ed. Susan Broomhall (Amsterdam, 2018), pp. 309–34
—, 'La Fin du règne de François Ier et l'avènement d'Henri II d'après les
    dèpêches de Jean de Saint-Mauris (1547)', Cour de France, article
    2749, www.cour-de-france.fr, accessed 10 December 2024
Predonzani, Massimo, and Vicenzo Alberici, *The Italian Wars*, vol. III:
    Francis I and the Battle of Pavia 1525 (Warwick, 2022)
Prys, Morgan, 'Un chroniqueur gallois à Calais', *Revue du Nord*, XLVII/185
    (April–June 1965), pp. 195–202
Rentet, Thierry, 'Network Mapping: Ties of Fidelity and Dependency
    among the Major Domestic Officers of Anne de Montmorency',
    French History, XVII/2 (2003), pp. 109–26
—, *Anne de Montmorency, Grand Maître de François Ier* (Rennes, 2011)
Richardson, Glenn, 'Entertainments for the French Ambassadors at
    the Court of Henry VIII', *Renaissance Studies*, IX/4 (1995), pp. 404–15
—, 'The Privy Chamber of Henry VIII and Anglo-French Relations
    1515–1520', *Court Historian*, IV/2 (1999), pp. 119–40
—, *Renaissance Monarchy: The Reigns of Henry VIII, Francis I and Charles V*
    (London, 2002)
—, 'Eternal Peace, Occasional War: Anglo-French Relations under
    Henry VIII', in *Tudor England and Its Neighbours*, ed. S. Doran and
    G. Richardson (Basingstoke, 2005), pp. 44–73

—, 'The French Connection: Francis I and England's Break with Rome', in *'The Contending Kingdoms': France and England, 1420–1700*, ed. Glenn Richardson (Aldershot, 2008), pp. 95–116

—, *The Field of Cloth of Gold* (New Haven, CT, and London, 2013)

—, 'Boys and Their Toys: Kingship, Masculinity and Material Culture in the Sixteenth Century', in *The Image and Perception of Monarchy in Medieval and Early Modern Europe*, ed. Sean McGlynn and Elena Woodacre (Newcastle upon Tyne, 2014), pp. 183–206

—, *Wolsey* (New Haven, CT, and London, 2020)

Rothstein, Marian, 'Homer for the Court of François I', *Renaissance Quarterly*, LIX/3 (2006), pp. 732–67

Russell, Joycelyne G., *Peacemaking in the Renaissance* (London, 1986)

Sainte-Marie, Père Anselme de, *Histoire généalogique et chronologique de la maison royale de France, des pairs, des grands officiers de la Couronne et de la Maison du Roy . . .*, 9 vols (Paris, 1726–33)

Scailliérez, Cécile, *François Ier et ses artistes dans les collections du Louvre* (Paris, 1992)

Scarisbrick, Jack J., *Henry VIII* (London, 1968)

Schneebalg-Perelman, Sophie, 'Richesses du garde-meuble parisien de François Ier, inventaires inédits de 1542 et 1551', *Gazette des Beaux-Arts*, LXXVIII (1971), pp. 253–304

Stephenson, Barbara M., *The Power and Patronage of Marguerite de Navarre* (Aldershot, 2004)

Toesca, Ilaria, 'Silver in the Time of François Ier: A New Identification', *Apollo*, XC (October 1969), pp. 292–7

Vatin, Nicolas, 'The Ottoman View of France from the Late Fifteenth to the Mid-Sixteenth Century', *French History*, XXIX/10 (2015), pp. 6–11

Walsby, Malcolm, *The Counts of Laval: Culture, Patronage and Religion in Fifteenth- and Sixteenth-Century France* (Aldershot, 2007)

Wellman, Kathleen, *Queens and Mistresses of Renaissance France* (New Haven, CT, and London, 2013)

ACKNOWLEDGEMENTS

I would like to thank friends – both academic and personal – who have shared and informed my interest in Francis I of France over the years, and who have encouraged my work on him. I am grateful to the late Robert Jean Knecht for his expert guidance and assistance when I first began researching Francis as part of my doctoral research on Anglo-French relations, and for his friendship thereafter. My scholarly debts to experts on the period are many, but I would particularly like to thank Mark Bryant, Stuart Carroll, Tony Claydon, Susan Doran, Charles Giry-Deloison, Mark Greengrass, Mary Hollingsworth, Cédric Michon, John Murphy, David Potter, Penny Roberts and David Starkey for their insights and support over many years. I would like also to thank Donald McPhail for reading the text. I thank Michael Leaman at Reaktion for the opportunity to write this book, and Amy Salter and her production team. I am grateful to my colleagues at St Mary's University for a sabbatical term that enabled me to work on this and other projects, my students at St Mary's, and those whom I have taught through the Oxford University Department for Continuing Education. Finally, I wish to remember the late Roger Mettam as a friend and mentor, whose deep understanding of the way early modern French monarchy worked informed and shaped my own. This book is dedicated to him.

PHOTO ACKNOWLEDGEMENTS

The author and publishers wish to express their thanks to the sources listed below for illustrative material and/or permission to reproduce it. Some locations of artworks are also given below, in the interest of brevity:

AdobeStock: pp. 38 (guitou60), 119 (sissoupitch); Bibliothèque nationale de France, Paris: pp. 26 (MS Français 143, fol. 1r), 49; Bridgeman Images: pp. 46 (British Library, London – Harley MS 6205, fol. 3r), 96 (Musée Condé, Chantilly), 139, 164 (photo © Raffaello Bencini), 186; The British Museum, London: p. 83; The Cleveland Museum of Art, OH: p. 140; The Fitzwilliam Museum, Cambridge: 156; Hampton Court Palace – Royal Collection Trust/© His Majesty King Charles III 2025: p. 64; The Metropolitan Museum of Art, New York: pp. 15, 18, 30, 135, 143; Musée Condé, Chantilly: pp. 6, 43, 191 (MS 721, fol. 1v); Musée du Louvre, Paris: pp. 60, 92, 122, 172; The National Archives, Kew: p. 99 (E30-1109); National Galleries of Scotland, Edinburgh: pp. 74, 114; Nationalmuseum, Stockholm/Erik Cornelius: p. 85; Philadelphia Museum of Art, PA: p. 106; Wikimedia Commons: p. 10 (photo Myrabella, CC BY-SA 4.0).

INDEX

Page numbers in *italics* refer to illustrations